REDISCOVERING WONDER
Putting God at the Center of Worship

by David Gipson

REDISCOVERING WONDER:
Putting God at the Center of Worship
Copyright (c) 2024 by David Gipson

www.DaveGipson.net

*For my fellow worship leaders,
choir members, band instrumentalists,
vocalists, and tech team members.*

*Keep fighting the good fight,
and I hope this book helps you, like David,
to be "even more undignified than this"
(2 Samuel 6:22)*

*Love,
Dave*

CONTENTS

Prelude - 6

Deconstructing Worship - 9

A Love Story - 15

God-Centered Worship - 26

Practically Worship - 36

Inside Out Worship - 44

A Worshipping Church - 49

Sacred Cows and Camel Tipping - 58

Divine Mistakes - 64

"I See Dead People" - 70

The Old Razzle Dazzle - 81

The Power of a Worshipping Choir - 88

Standing in the (generation) Gap - 96

The Problem of Intimacy - 101

Creative Differences - 107

Strange Fire - 113

Lowering Your Shields - 119

How Much "Freedom of Worship" is Too Much? - 126

Raiders of the Lost Ark – 130

Talent's Not Enough - 136

About Dave - 142

PRELUDE

One of the saddest parts of adulthood is losing your childhood sense of wonder.

It's fun at first to be the one who notices the Wizard hiding behind the curtain, pulling the levers. We'd love to figure out the trick to the magic illusion we just saw performed. But the older I get, the less anything surprises me. And that's sad.

After all the curtains are pulled back and the tricks are revealed, we're only left with one thing in this world that still provides that sense of wonder: God. He's the last stop on the wonder train. Thankfully, He's provided a way that we can weekly experience Him in all His wonder.

That place is church. And when His people really praise Him, God "inhabits the praises of His people" (Psalm 22:3). When He inhabits those praises, we experience "fullness of joy" in His presence (Psalm 16:11). All the wonders of childhood we lost are very much alive in Him whose right hand offers us "pleasures forevermore".

Who in their right mind would pass up that offer? But I can remember how I almost did…

I remember once praying to God, "Lord, I'll do anything you want me to do. But please, don't ask me to be a worship leader!" The reason was, in my experience growing up in church, it seemed like the most boring job possible.

Why? How could experiencing the God of the Universe possibly be boring? Because worship seemed to have little purpose in the churches I attended. It was something we did but were never told why. And as far as entertainment value, I found little in the syrupy-slow hymns and the flowery, silly solos.

Yep, I'm thinking of you, *"The Holy City"*:

> *"…me thought the voice of angels, from heaven in answer, rang"*

"Me thought"? Seriously? This stuff was kryptonite for a teenage boy!

I surrendered to vocational ministry and waited to see what God would do. Surprisingly, He sent the music of Keith Green to awaken me to the vast possibilities of Christian music. And one crazy night, my youth leader took me to an Andrae Crouch concert. Worship suddenly became an experience like no other, where God Himself seemed to show up and fill the room with electricity.

Over the next years, I served multiple churches and saw lots of changes in style and function. I've watched worship music go from just one offshoot of a much larger Contemporary Christian Music industry to basically becoming the "last man standing" today. In the late 2000s, Christian music companies, along with many church choral companies, started imploding. Then, with the Covid pandemic, many of those companies who'd supplied choral music to churches simply vanished.

It's been quite a ride, but I'm still here, leading worship every Sunday. Everything has changed, and yet, much of what really matters has never changed…

God is still on His throne, and his right hand still holds those pleasures forevermore. He deserves to be worshipped, enthusiastically, lavishly, and unendingly!

With this book, I hope to answer for you my questions about worship that began as a boy in a Baptist church in the south. There is indeed a reason for our worship, and a point to our praise. And as it turns out, there's really nothing else we're doing right now that will matter more a hundred years from now.

Make that "a thousand years from now". Because the wonder is still with us today, waiting for us to return to real worship.

DECONSTRUCTING WORSHIP

Seriously, when was the last time you heard someone say something positive about their church's worship music?

I don't blame them. There's no surer way to get myself in a deep funk (and I don't mean the musical kind) than to watch some church's live stream on Sunday afternoon after my own worship leading is over.

And sometimes, the service that depresses me is my own. Everybody has bad days, for sure. The fact of the matter is worship leading is a tough job. You never, ever make everyone happy. And if you make pleasing everyone your goal, you will be certain never to please God.

That is just one of the many problems with trying to lead worship in an evangelical church.

The problem often is that some of us really don't get worship at all. Sure, some services suffer from untalented or unqualified personnel. But many of our services betray the fact that when it comes to worship, we've completely missed the point.

One problem is churches often approach worship not primarily based on Scriptural content, but on human preference and musical style. While this shouldn't be the case, we do have to admit that style and human preferences matter. They simply shouldn't be ALL that matters!

So that's another problem – balancing the priority of Scriptural fidelity with the human desire for music we enjoy.

Styles in popular music continually change, and this naturally affects the music in our churches. Songs are an important part of worship – they are the tools we give the congregation to worship with. Just as the wrong tool can create disfunction with a household chore, the wrong songs can make it difficult for a congregation to effectively enter into worship.

A Gregorian chant might have worked very well several hundred years ago, but today's congregation will be hard-pressed to sing along with you in Latin. Likewise, the latest Christian R&B song may have scriptural lyrics, but a predominantly senior adult congregation will be giving you some passionate feedback at the end of the service.

So musical style does indeed matter. BUT…it should not matter most.

Got it? Yeah, it's quite the balancing act.

The seniors complain we're not doing enough hymns, so we create a "traditional service" to make them happy. We make the other service the "contemporary service", and most of the young adults gravitate to it.

Everybody's happy, right?

Not really. These services also divide the congregation along generational lines and inhibit healthy fellowship between those generations. They disconnect seniors from the new life that new worship songs represent – the "new wineskins" of what God is doing now in the church. They also separate the young adults from hundreds of years of tradition. Their kids don't hear the songs that sustained their grandparents through seasons of struggle and tragedy. Their worship lacks gravitas and foundation: it's only as good as the latest disposable pop anthem.

Drastically separating worship styles undercuts one of the important strengths of a multi-generational church. It disconnects seniors from the enthusiasm of young adults, while disconnecting young adults from the wisdom and experience of seniors. A congregation given inherent balance by God is divided into two separate UNbalanced congregations, each tipping dangerously in opposite directions.

Am I blaming pastors for separating services by style? Not at all! They're doing it for the same reason God finally gave in to Israel's complaining and gave them a king – to shut them up! The congregation's unwillingness to die to self and think of the needs the other generations have made the unhealthy compromise necessary. Seriously, we should be ashamed.

If not "traditional" and "contemporary" services, what do we do?

Well, of course the answer must then be a "blended service", where we will do BOTH hymns and new worship choruses in hopes this will make everybody happy. The reality is they often make both sides even more dissatisfied.

In most blended services, we choose a quota of hymns that are given new contemporary arrangements. Often, these arrangements make those beloved hymns mostly unsingable for seniors. Likewise, the new worship chorus arrangements are homogenized to sound like the "Muzac" one might hear in an elevator or dentist's office. Those church orchestras, usually consisting of a bunch of high school level woodwind and brass players, drain all the life and power out of what were guitar-based songs.

Remembering hearing "Stairway To Heaven" played by Mantovani's stringed orchestra? Exciting stuff, right?

This is about where most church pastors throw up their hands, throw in the towel and just settle for whatever they've been doing. Or they overreact and fire the worship leader in hopes that some new person will be the magical hire that makes everyone happy.

Good luck with that. But maybe what we need is to step back a minute and remind ourselves what really matters in worship.

What matters is God. What He wants. What pleases Him. What draws His presence. We must put Him first and make sure he stays there in our hearts. Because when style is our chief focus, man is the one on the throne of worship. Not God.

In deconstructing our worship, we need to ask ourselves some tough questions about our church's worship.

Is our worship man-centered, or God-centered?

> Do we really believe Kierkegaard's example for Biblical worship, in that we view God as the true audience, and those on the platform merely the prompters for the congregation's performance? Or have we switched places and put people as the audience, the worship leaders as the performers, and God is left outside doing parking lot ministry?

Does our worship give the congregation tools (songs) with which they can easily use to engage in worship?

> Are the songs not only Scriptural but also easy to sing? Do we introduce new songs in a way people can easily learn them? Do we show respect to seniors by incorporating hymns from their past?

Does our worship represent the full gamut of human emotion, or just one safe emotionless plane?

> Will people experience joy, lament, passion, and desire during our services? Or will we just stick to the medium-tempo, dispassionate but Scriptural centerground? If we do, should we expect people from other worship backgrounds (and ethnicities) to feel included in our services?

Is the congregation included in worship and encouraged to participate, or are they given a free pass to spectate on the sidelines?

> Do we actively encourage people to sing, to clap, to lift hands, and other Biblical expressions of worship during our services? Are there seasons of prayer where they can express their need for intercession from brothers and sisters in the congregation? Or should they have just stayed home and watched the livestream?

Most churches I know need to start asking these questions and "deconstructing" their worship. They need to put the man-centered questions of style aside for a while, and first make sure our hearts are in the right place and God is in His right place.

Frankly, it's not OK that we're about to lose several hundred years' worth of hymns. They are an important part of our spiritual heritage. Many hymns need to be preserved so we can remember who we are and from where we came. But it's also not ok to ignore God's command to "sing to the Lord a NEW song". And it's not OK that prayer is relegated to a perfunctory task, often delivered devoid of purpose or passion.

Our worship needs to reflect not only the God of Scripture but also the people gathered to worship Him. We need to incorporate a variety of musical styles, as opposed to everything sounding the same in a service. We should be using different instrumentation to create different moods. And passion must be an essential ingredient of our worship.

If we aren't hungering and thirsting after God, we should not expect Him to be drawn to our services.

In fact, we may not be the only ones dissatisfied with our worship today…

> *"I can't stand your religious meetings. I'm fed up with your conferences and conventions. I want nothing to do with your religion projects, your pretentious slogans and goals. I'm sick of your fund-raising schemes, your public relations and image making. I've had all I can take of your noisy ego-music. When was the last time you sang to me?"*
> - Amos 5:21 and following (The Message)

Maybe we're dissatisfied because His Spirit is within us, and He's dissatisfied too. Let's allow Him to tip over the tables of our temples if He chooses. It may stir up some dust in the process, but God's presence in our worship will be more than worth the trouble.

Because if God's presence isn't there, is it really worship? That's the most important question of all.

A LOVE STORY

Most of us know worship from the church we grew up in, and I'm no exception. I remember the Organ prelude, the Call to Worship by the choir, the hymns, the Welcome (turn around and shake hands with people like you care). There was some sort of choir anthem and a solo we called the "Special Music" (to differentiate is from the other "not so special music"). Then a sermon, and sometimes even a choral response ("The Lord is in His Holy Temple" was a popular one). Then the invitation, benediction, and organ postlude.

There was nothing wrong with any of that. The one thing I never knew was "why" we did things that way. In fact, I grew up in what was considered a Bible-believing, Bible teaching church from as long as I can remember. But I don't remember one single sermon on what worship was, and why we should do it a certain way.

No, we just did it. We had no idea what we were doing exactly, or why we were supposed to be singing. But everyone else was, so we pretended to, at least.

I think it would be wise here at the front of my little book that we take the advice of Julie Andrews to the Von Trapp kids and "start at the very beginning" …

First, worship is a verb. It's something you do.

It's not something you just sit back and observe. it's not something you watch on livestream while doing dishes. It's something you actively participate in, or else it's only religious entertainment for you.

> "Jesus answered him, "The first of all the commandments is: 'Hear, O Israel, the LORD our God, the LORD is one. And you shall love the LORD your God with **all your heart, with all your soul, with all your mind, and with all your strength.** This is the first commandment." – Mark 12:29-30

If you do something with all your "heart, soul, mind, and strength", there's a good chance you won't be passive about it. It is something you're doing with enthusiasm. And it's easy to be enthusiastic about something you love.

Just watch people at any sporting event. Lots of passion and enthusiasm.

> *"Bless the LORD, O my soul; and **all that is within me**, bless His holy name!* – Psalm 103:1

Here again, if I do something with "all that's within me", I'm giving it all I've got. I'm holding nothing back. As the kids would say, I'm "all in".

Second, to build on worship as something you do, the Biblical descriptions of worship make it clear it's actually a "contact sport". It is a very tactile, physical expression of passion for God employing my mind, BODY, and spirit. Look at this listing of the Biblical "postures of praise":

Lifting up our hands
(Ps. 63:4, 134:2, 141:2, 1 Tim 2:8)

Clapping
(Ps. 47:1)

Playing of instruments
(Ps. 33:2-3, 57:9, 150:3-5)

Standing
(2 Chron 5:12, Ps. 135:2, Rev 4:9-11)

Kneeling, bowing, prostration
(Ps. 95:6, Rev 19:4, Eph 3:14, Phil 2:10-11, Neh 8:6)

Singing
(Ps. 47:6)

Audible
(Ps. 26:7, 66:8, 17, 98:4, Acts 16:25)

Dancing, leaping
(Ps. 30:11, 149:3, 150:4, Ex 15:20-21, Acts 3:8)

Shouting
(Ps. 47:1, 35:27)

Crying out
(Isa 12:6, Ps. 89:26)

Singing in the Spirit
(1 Cor 14:15)

One thing that was drummed into my head as a church kid was how the sermon was everything. Nothing mattered more in a worship service than the sermon, because it was proclamation of the "Word of God". The implication was the music was just the preliminaries and the sermon was all that mattered. However, the following verse seems to contradict that assumption:

"David and the captains of the army separated for the service some of the sons of Asaph, of Heman, and of Jeduthun, who should prophesy with harps, stringed instruments, and cymbals" - 1 Chronicles 25:1

This passage says that the King had appointed the captains of his army to choose who the worship leaders would be! Worship must be of great importance if the Joint Chiefs of Staff are picking them. Also noticed they were called to "prophecy" on their instruments, not just play them. They were proclaiming the Word of God the same as any preacher would, except the only difference was theirs was done with a melody and rhythm.

Here are a few more significant Biblical passages referring to worship and praise:

2 Chronicles 20:19 Then the Levites of the children of the Kohathites and of the children of the Korahites stood up to **praise** the LORD God of Israel with voices loud and high.

2 Chronicles 20:22 Now when they began to sing and to praise, the LORD set ambushes against the people of Ammon, Moab, and Mount Seir, who had come against Judah; and they were defeated. (worship as spiritual warfare)

Ezra 3:11 And they sang responsively, praising and giving thanks to the LORD: "For He is good, For His mercy endures forever toward Israel." Then all the people shouted with a great shout, when they praised the LORD, because the foundation of the house of the LORD was laid.

Psalm 9:1 I will praise You, O LORD, with my whole heart; I will tell of all Your marvelous works.

Psalm 16:11 You will show me the path of life; In Your presence is fullness of joy; At Your right hand are pleasures forevermore.

Psalm 22:3 But thou art holy, O thou that inhabitest the praises of Israel.

Psalm 22:25 My praise shall be of You in the great assembly; I will pay My vows before those who fear Him.

Psalm 28:7 The LORD is my strength and my shield; My heart trusted in Him, and I am helped; Therefore my heart greatly rejoices, And with my song I will praise Him.

Psalm 30:9 What profit is there in my blood, When I go down to the pit? Will the dust praise You? Will it declare Your truth?

Psalm 34:1 I will bless the LORD at all times; His praise shall continually be in my mouth.

Psalm 40:3 He has put a new song in my mouth—Praise to our God; Many will see it and fear, and will trust in the LORD.

Psalm 96:1 Oh, sing to the LORD a new song! Sing to the LORD, all the earth.

Psalm 100:4 Enter into His gates with thanksgiving, And into His courts with praise. Be thankful to Him, and bless His name. (This is a road map for entering into God's presence)

Psalm 138:2 I will worship toward Your holy temple, and praise Your name For Your lovingkindness and Your truth; For You have magnified Your word above all Your name.

Psalm 145:4 One generation shall praise Your works to another, and shall declare Your mighty acts. (A prescription for multigenerational worship)

Psalm 149:3 Let them praise His name with the dance; Let them sing praises to Him with the timbrel and harp.

Psalm 150:2 Praise Him for His mighty acts; Praise Him according to His excellent greatness!

Psalm 150:3 Praise Him with the sound of the trumpet; Praise Him with the lute and harp!

Psalm 150:5 Praise Him with loud cymbals; Praise Him with clashing cymbals!

Psalm 150:6 Let everything that has breath praise the LORD. Praise the LORD!

Isaiah 60:18 Violence shall no longer be heard in your land, Neither wasting nor destruction within your borders; But you shall call your walls Salvation, And your gates Praise.

Isaiah 66:1 Thus says the LORD: "Heaven is My throne, and earth is My footstool. Where is the house that you will build Me? And where is the place of My rest?"

Jeremiah 17:26 And they shall come from the cities of Judah and from the places around Jerusalem, from the land of Benjamin and from the lowland, from the mountains and from the South, bringing burnt offerings and sacrifices, grain offerings and incense, bringing sacrifices of praise to the house of the LORD.

Habakkuk 3:17-18 Though the fig tree may not blossom, Nor fruit be on the vines; Though the labor of the olive may fail, And the fields yield no food; Though the flock may be cut off from the fold, And there be no herd in the stalls— Yet I will rejoice in the LORD, I will joy in the God of my salvation.

John 4:23 But the hour is coming, and now is, when the true worshipers will worship the Father in spirit and truth; for the Father is seeking such to worship Him.

John 4:24 God is Spirit, and those who worship Him must worship in spirit and truth.

Acts 16:25 But at midnight Paul and Silas were praying and singing hymns to God, and the prisoners were listening to them.

1 Corinthians 14:26 How is it then, brethren? Whenever you come together, each of you has a psalm, has a teaching, has a tongue, has a revelation, has an interpretation. Let all things be done for edification.

Ephesians 5:19 Speaking to one another in psalms and hymns and spiritual songs, singing and making melody in your heart to the Lord

Colossians 3:16 Let the word of Christ dwell in you richly in all wisdom, teaching and admonishing one another in psalms and **hymns** and spiritual songs, singing with grace in your hearts to the Lord.

Hebrews 13:15 Therefore by Him let us continually offer the sacrifice of praise to God, that is, the fruit of our lips, giving thanks to His name.

You may have noticed there are many more passages in the Old Testament about worship than the New. I think there are some practical reasons for that.

First, the New Testament's "psalms, hymns and spiritual songs" descriptors seem to be a deconstruction itself of everything that was going on in the Old Testament. Paul is not ruling everything else out but boiling everything down into those basic three.

However, nothing about the New Testament teachings on worship contradict Old Testament teachings about worship. The simplification of New Testament teaching was probably essential considering that the venues of New Testament worship demanded the basics. When you move from Old Testament worship in temples led by hundreds of participants to worship in houses led by laypeople, you simply must get more basic. The only thing that's changed from the Old to the New is the administration, organizational structure, and perhaps the number of participants leading worship.

In contrast, Calvin's reductionist "regulative principle of worship" proposed we're only allowed to use practices that are implicitly mentioned in the New Testament in our worship. When taken to its extreme, this is how Church of Christ believers justify keeping musical instruments out of worship. They aren't mentioned in the New Testament, but that's because they would not have been present in most of the homes where the church was meeting.

If you wanted to take that principle to its most ridiculous natural conclusion, iPads and indoor bathrooms should also be prohibited during a worship service since they're not mentioned in the New Testament! However, there is no New Testament warning against stringed instruments or expanding to other kinds of worship. Therefore, incorporation of new forms of worship and new tools and instruments for worship is reasonable and completely Biblical.

Of all the passages in the Bible on worship, there is one I believe is most pertinent to us in the 21st century church:

I sleep, but my heart is awake; It is the voice of my beloved! He knocks, saying, "Open for me, my sister, my love, My dove, my perfect one; For my head is covered with dew, My locks with the drops of the night."

I have taken off my robe; How can I put it on again? I have washed my feet; How can I defile them? - Song of Solomon 5:2-3

While this passage may seem an odd choice, I picked it to point out a key thing about the Bible most people miss. The Bible is not primarily a theology book, history book, or a rule book.

The Bible is a love story. Why else would God call His church "the bride of Christ"?

It is a story of the greatest love the world has ever known, and how we were created to recognize God's loveliness and acknowledge it. Our very purpose on earth is praise, as the Westminster Catechism accurately reflects:

> *"Q. What is the chief end of man?* A. Man's chief end is to glorify God, and to enjoy him forever."

While God is not needy, God desires for His creation to see Him and respond to His beauty and love. And worship is our "love language" toward God:

Therefore by Him let us continually offer the sacrifice of praise to God, that is, the fruit of our lips, giving thanks to His name. - Hebrews 13:15

God responds to your passion for Him with His presence. God is the pursuer, constantly pursuing His beloved:

But the hour is coming, and now is, when the true worshipers will worship the Father in spirit and truth; **for the Father is seeking such to worship Him.** *- John 4:23*

And so…

Adam walking in the garden
Enoch walked with God
Abraham was the "friend of God"

But like Adam, our hearts are bound to wander to other loves. And God is jealous of our infidelity.

So Job was tested to see if he loved God more than God's blessings.

So God warned us to "have no other gods before Him".

So the idols in the temple of Dagon fell down before the Ark of the Covenant.

So God set up a Tabernacle, where He could once again have a rendezvous with His creation. But the tent is divided up in sections - holy place divided from Most Holy Place - like an unfaithful spouse banished to the far end of the house. Moses respected God's warnings about breaching the protocol of the separations.

But then David, a "man after God's heart", sets up a different Tabernacle for worship. Where Moses emphasized the holiness and separateness of God, David emphasized touching God's heart, through worship.

In his Tabernacle, worship was playing 24/7, constantly lifting up praise to God.

In his Tabernacle, there was no veil of separation between the worshippers and the Ark of God's presence.

In his Tabernacle, there was no blood sacrifice.

David broke all the rules and sat before the Ark. But he knew a secret about God, that His desire was for our worship. He gave God what He desired, and God gave David intimacy in His presence.

But after David, the veil goes back up.

God tells Hosea, "You want to know how I feel about my people's betrayal? Go marry a prostitute and you'll know!" Finally, after Malachi there are 400 years of silence…

…until Jesus!

That is why the veil was torn down in the Temple when Jesus was crucified. God always hated that separation between us. And now that Jesus had paid our debt of sin, we could have unhindered fellowship once again. The romance was repaired!

And now today, in our hearts God is rebuilding that Tabernacle of David…

'After this I will return and will rebuild the tabernacle of David, which has fallen down; I will rebuild its ruins, And I will set it up; So that the rest of mankind may seek the Lord, Even all the Gentiles who are called by My name, Says the Lord who does all these things.' - Acts 15:16-17

Now His Spirit actually resides inside of us. So when all God's children gather together, it is the culmination of a great love story. We join our voices together, celebrating the great God who sought us while in our sin, rescued us and made us His Bride.

Sadly, today many churches keep the presence of God outside their worship services. Sometimes it's out of fear, that God may inspire us to respond to Him in some embarrassing way. Our intimidation at expressing intimacy and affection in worship must grieve Him so, as we insist on going through the motions Sunday after Sunday…

Behold, I stand at the door and knock. If anyone hears My voice and opens the door, I will come in to him and dine with him, and he with Me. - Revelation 3:20

This is why worship matters. Each Sunday we gather together once again to tell the grand love story that weaves throughout Scripture. And this is why we can't help but praise Him!

GOD-CENTERED WORSHIP

There was a great deal of talk over the past 30+ years about churches becoming more "seeker-sensitive". That meant we needed to remove impediments to worship that were keeping non-Christians (or "seekers") away. It often involved removing things off-putting to seekers from worship that were deemed nonessentials. So churches removed offering plates and used offering boxes in the lobby that were easier for seekers to walk past without guilt. Suits were traded in by pastors for more casual attire. Organs were dumped for guitars and drums.

Though met by some with great consternation, none of these changes constituted unfaithfulness to the Biblical concept of worship. Some may have even helped more authentic worship happen in certain environments. However, while everyone was asking "what do seekers want" or "what do church members want", there was one question people often forgot to ask:

"What does GOD want from our worship services?"

While I can agree we need to remove any man-made stumbling block to people coming to Christ, worship must first be sensitive to what God wants. That's because worship is, by definition, about God, to God, and for God! If He is not pleased, has worship even really happened?

Much like the tree falling unheard in a forest, if we sing songs but God refuses to listen, have we really worshipped?

There is nothing more important in the life of a Christian than worship. While prayer, Bible study, and witnessing are important disciplines of the mature Christian life, they can become hollow, legalistic exercises without the oil of worship. However, for most Christians worship is approached rather casually, as if it's just something we do because there's nothing good on Sunday morning TV. And because many are neglecting God's desires in worship, too many churches are now suffering and dying.

The remedy to the sickness in our churches is to practice God-Centered worship. Worship God accepts will revive and resurrect many of our churches, and from the number of church closures we currently face, it couldn't happen any faster. We need to ask ourselves what God wants from our worship before our churches become spiritual deserts and historical relics.

"Man-Centered" Vs. "God-Centered" Worship

You get something totally different in worship when you realize God is supposed to be the audience and not people.

WHEN WORSHIP IS MAN-CENTERED…
- *We are in charge, not God*
- *What we can achieve is only the sum of our own efforts*
- *Even when we succeed, real joy is not present*
- *Our talents receive the glory*
- *But those talents ultimately fall short of their full potential*
- *We're fueled by fear of man's rejection*

But when pleasing God is the focus, the difference is in the results:

WHEN WORSHIP IS GOD-CENTERED...
- *We function in our giftedness*
- *We are less self-serving and man-honoring*
- *God moves despite our level of ability*
- *Fear of failure is absent as desire to please God becomes primary*
- *Getting the credit is not only unimportant, but discouraged*
- *The end result goes far beyond the abilities of the individual*

IN GOD-CENTERED WORSHIP, THE CONGREGATION PARTICIPATES

I've known people who say, "Although I just stand quietly during the worship services, I still worship in my own way." I agree that you cannot determine the spiritual temperature of a believer by how energetic they are in worship. But most every reference in the Bible to Worship and Praise involves the worshipper *doing something*. In the Bible, they sang, or clapped, or shouted. They lifted hands, knelt, or occasionally fell prostrate. Meditation and silent prayer was also a part of worship, but was done in expectation of God speaking and never in lieu of active participation.

Biblical worship is, by nature, overt, demonstrative, and proactive. Never does the Bible say, "Give glory to God with your passive resignation". Being nonplussed and underwhelmed are not valid responses to the presence of an awesome God.

Worship was never meant to be a "spectator sport", where the congregation just looks on. Our Father not only desires the worship of those on the platform who sing or play, He also wants unashamed worship from each of His children in the congregation. Each person's worship is precious to Him, with each one giving praise with their own unique way.

But you may say, "Aren't you judging others who may not be as animated as you? How can you know their hearts?"

Of course not, I can't. I do know people are "wired" quite differently when it comes to expressing emotions. My wife is what most people would call "even-tempered". Her highs are not too high, and her lows are mostly undetectable. I envy her "smooth sailing" nature, and often wish I could trade with her. I am the emotional one in our family. So while Dawn will hear a certain song and respond with a pleasant smile, you may look over and see me blubbering like a baby.

Does my emotion mean I love Jesus more than my wife does? Of course not. People respond to God differently. We express the very same love and passion for God in our own unique ways. But individuality can never be an excuse for not participating in worship. God wants praise from each of us, and it's our individuality that makes it special, no matter how elaborate or subdued.

But…we must do something. Doing nothing in response to a magnificent God is not an option.

IN "GOD-CENTERED" WORSHIP, THERE IS FREEDOM

There are as many different ways to worship as there are worshippers. Each believer expresses his or her love for the Lord somewhat differently. But the one ingredient that must be in every worship service of every church is freedom. Each one of us must be free to worship in the way God is leading us, within the specific boundaries dictated by Scripture.

We must allow God to create an environment in worship where each believer feels the freedom to express what is in his or her heart to God. But I have found that this level of freedom is especially hard for most men. Some may tell you worship is just not a "guy thing", but some men simply do not feel free to express their love for God with any emotion.

In fact, men are actually pretty emotional, when given permission to be. You've seen them on the tee ball field with a bunch of 6-year-olds playing a game, not even keeping score. Still, some dad will be screaming his head off at the ref who called his kid "out". I've seen tears, screams, and jumping in the air from men. Someone told them it was ok to do those things in sports.

How could God deserve any less passion from you than you would give a football team? He deserves your enthusiasm. Real worship encompasses the whole person, including the full range of their human emotions. For years we've assumed showing a full range of emotions in church is inappropriate, but that is not what the Bible says.

If you ever want to take an emotional roller coaster ride, just read what a great warrior like David wrote in the Psalms. David poured out his whole heart upon the Lord in worship, and God deserves nothing less from each of us. Yet the same man who acts like a lunatic when his college team wins on Saturday will sit comatose during worship on Sunday! We are afraid: afraid of what others will think, afraid that what we will do will be misinterpreted. And that fear keeps us from worshipping the way we truly desire. This grieves the heart of God, because He desires us to worship that way too.

Some hide behind denominational monikers so we can have a "pass" from freedom in worship. "It's just not part of our religious tradition to be expressive," we say. But no matter what church you're in, God expects your congregation to encourage Biblical expressions of praise within your worship services. If what the Bible says is against your church's rules, then your church needs to change! A church that limits that expression to singing only is a church that is limiting how its people can bless God…and how God will bless them in return.

For years, I stiff-armed God with my involvement in praise because I didn't want people to think I was a "holy roller". I remain a happy Southern Baptist today, but I have to admit we have let the excesses of a few keep many of us frozen like dead men in our pews. Our fear of excess has allowed the pendulum to swing to the extreme of dry and barren formality. We have made "dignity" and "appropriateness" the hills our churches will die on. And believe me, they're dying fast.

What many of us call dignity in worship may actually be spiritual rigor mortise setting in. We need to die to our dignity and worship the Lord with the humility of little children again.

IN "GOD-CENTERED" WORSHIP, WE ARE MINISTERING TO GOD

The most amazing fallacy about worship today is that we believers think it must be done to our liking. How funny that we could make worship about us, when it is all about us ministering to God. How strange to take the one truly special thing that we can do to bless God and do it specifically so it will bless us.

I learned so much about God's desire for our worship when I became a father. The most wonderful experience I have with my children is when they say, "Daddy, I love you", and they cuddle up in my lap. God encouraged us to address Him as "Abba Father", which would be the equivalent of saying "Daddy" in our culture. God is saying that He desires the same intimacy and tenderness with us that a father desires from His children.

Your individual worship, embodying all the nuance and uniqueness of who you are, is your best gift to God as His child. You may do other acts of service, such as giving to the poor, teaching a Bible class, or visiting the sick, but those things will never replace the gift of your voice lifted in song, your hands raised in praise. But some Christians seem to be saying, "I'll give you my life and my service. But please keep your distance, God. I'm not willing to risk showing you how I feel about you in front of everybody else."

Of all the things we can do in the name of Jesus, the one thing that ministers solely to God is worship. Feeding the poor or teaching a class is part of our spiritual worship, sure. But when we do those things, we are mainly blessing the church. When we worship, our focus is on blessing only the Lord. Worship is the one gift we can give to God and God alone!

IN "GOD-CENTERED" WORSHIP, OUR PRAISE IS IMPORTANT

I was listening to Dr. David Jeremiah preach recently, and I will never forget his response to a couple of his church members. In complimenting him on how great his preaching was, they told him, "We love your preaching so much, we don't even come for the music part of the service. All we show up for is the sermon!" The pastor looked sadly at the couple and said, "If you are skipping everything in the service except for my sermon, then my preaching hasn't done you much good!" In spite of their attempt to stroke his ego, Dr. Jeremiah really understood the importance of worship in the believer's life as well as in the Bible.

I don't think it's a coincidence that out of ten Commandments, the first, second, and fourth deal with areas of worship. God wanted us to see that worshipping Him was serious business. God took seven chapters in Leviticus just to tell how to organize the logistics of the worship area. Also, the Tabernacle of worship was placed in the center of encampment of God's people specifically to show that all of life should revolve around worship.

Worship is the one thing we are doing now that will continue throughout eternity. Since it will be God's priority for how we spend our days then, we ought to make it our priority now.

I had always thought that the first priority of the church was to win the lost. While this is certainly high on the list, God demands that we worship Him first of all. The Christian life is designed so that all our good works - witnessing, tithing, service - are meant to be an overflow from our worship life. Otherwise, even these necessary things become just dead works.

True obedience to God begins by bowing the whole person before God's throne as a living sacrifice. This is why Isaiah, after experiencing what was probably the ultimate in face-to-face worship with an awesome God, responded by saying "Here am I! Send me" (Isaiah 6). When we put worship in the right place, evangelism is a natural result of being in God's presence.

In Luke 10, we can all remember the story of Mary, who just wanted to be at Jesus' feet adoring Him, and Martha, who insisted on being church hostess for the day. When faced with Martha's rebuke for Mary's lack of assistance, Jesus said, "...only one thing is needed, and Mary has chosen the better." To put it more bluntly: God can live without your acts of service, but God wants you! I believe He would be saying to many of us "thanks so much for teaching that Sunday School class, singing in the choir, and the offering was nice, but ...could we just spend a little time together first?"

IN "GOD-CENTERED" WORSHIP, SPIRITUAL HEALING CAN BE EXPECTED

God's Word tells us to put on the "garment of praise for the spirit of heaviness." I believe much of the depression we see in fellow Christians is due to a lack of worship. If you ever stood on the platform at church and looked out, you'd be stunned at the large numbers of unhappy, unfulfilled, and just plain miserable people you'd see. And while some of them may have sins from which they have not repented, many of them are suffering because they do not know the healing power of worship in their lives.

One Sunday at the church I served in Tennessee, I did something that I had never done before in a worship service. As we were experiencing a time of intimate and passionate worship, I stopped the music and asked if there was anyone in the congregation who had a need only God could meet. Several hands went up around the auditorium. I then felt led to ask those people to come forward and kneel at the altar to pray. As I heard the words come out of my mouth, a rush of fear went through me as I wondered if anyone would respond.

We were not used to looking spiritually "needy" in our church. Spiritual "transparency" was not the norm, and I had no idea what would happen next. But to my amazement, first one…then another…then tens of people started streaming down the aisles to the altar. They were kneeling, some weeping openly, some by themselves and some in couples.

I then asked if our people would come and "lay hands" on the people at the altar! Laying on of hands was something that only happened during Deacon Ordination, when the older deacons would try to mess up the hair of the new rookies as much as possible. But I found out that night that it deeply ministers to people in a time of need.

This became something that the congregation urged me to continue in future service, and praying together over people in need at the altar became a regular part of our worship. Many times during these moments of altar ministry, I would feel a dear brother's hand on my shoulder and hear him speak my name to the Father. Even though by nature I am a loner and have been hurt in the past by people who abused my friendship, God made it clear to me in these worship times just how much I needed other people.

IN "GOD-CENTERED" WORSHIP, WE GAIN HIS PERSPECTIVE

In addition to ministering to the Lord, your worship has a residual effect on those around you, and especially upon the lost. While the worship service is meant for the Body of Christ to give pleasure to the Father, it also has the ability to show the world the life-changing power and joy that is found in the presence of the Lord. In passionate, God-sensitive worship, they will see that we really mean what we are saying about God. But emotionless, sterile worship will in turn inoculate them from catching what we have!

Worship takes our attention away from the problems that seem to be so insurmountable and focuses us on God - the ultimate solution to every problem. When we see Him in all of His power, we see how truly small our problems are in comparison. Worship is the great perspective-giver. We see the world, and our problems, from a "God's-eye view". And when God is put in His proper place, nothing else is really that important. When we stop focusing inward with self-pity and focus upward with worship, we see that nothing besides our relationship with God matters.

When we, as a congregation, decide to make worship a time of ministering to God instead of living up to the expectations of those around us, we will see His love poured out on us and our church in a way we never imagined. That's what happens every time when you put God at the center of your worship.

PRACTICALLY WORSHIP

"Worship is the missing jewel of the church."
A. W. Tozer

Tozer was right: worship really is the missing jewel of the church, at least for many churches I have seen. We have strategies galore for church growth, witnessing, and building campaigns; so much so that it's become impossible to keep up with the latest one.

We have focused on just about everything else in our churches, except worship.

In the midst of the enlightenment provided by books and seminars, worship has remained a troubling and divisive issue for many congregations. For example, I tried making a list of all the different styles of worship I've heard of in recent years:

"Seeker-sensitive"
"Seeker-driven"
"Gen-X worship"
"Ancient future"
"Contemporary"

"Blended"
"Traditional" or "Classic worship"

For most of us to choose a worship style would be like a farmer who stumbles into a Starbuck's looking for coffee. Just the list of options is confusing enough to make you swear off lattes for life!

Some pastors are also confused by worship, and the confusion is no accident. I believe that our enemy has hijacked the topic and fooled us into making secondary issues the main thing. So let's deal with a few practical basics about worship, and hopefully get some of the confusion out of the way.

Worship Styles

The style of worship we use actually is important, because the style used may limit what kind of people you will reach…or if you reach them at all. It will certainly affect how easily your present congregation enters into personal worship, because the musical style must be accessible to them most of the time.

The same way you would have difficulty singing along with songs written in a foreign language, musical styles are languages that speak to some people and not to others. Songs are one of the **tools** the worshipper is using to make contact with God in a service, so you definitely need to pick the right tools for the job.

But style is not the only issue, because God does not prefer one style of music over another. Contrary to what any music professional may think, God is not concerned with whether the music is "high-brow" or "low-brow". God is just as satisfied being worshipped through hymns, choruses, country music, classical, liturgical, as well as Latin Salsa. He loves it all, because it all represents the different people groups He loves.

When we embrace the fact that all styles are acceptable to God, we then can look clearly to determine what styles speak directly to our local congregation, and what styles don't. It is nice to stretch our congregations some by exposing them to new things and pushing the boundaries of their favorite styles. But our job is not to be "music educators", as some worship leaders choose to be. They set up one style of music as the "gold standard", and some push it on an unwilling congregation.

As much as I love classical music, it is not a style most people respond to in a worship setting. Yet I've known many a worship leader try and cram it down people's throats out of a musical snobbery. They're convinced that God prefers Bach and Handel to Gaither and Stamps Baxter. However, most of their people's hearts jump in delight when "Because He Lives" is sung, but they disengage during a Bach cantata.

We must decide if God has called us to be music educators or worship leaders. Are we leading people into God's presence or just pushing our own musical preferences on them?

Ultimately, **worship is meant to please God**. In all our discussions of style, this must be kept at the forefront of the discussion. Self-centered creatures that we are, we have taken something that was meant for His pleasure and made it all about us. As long as we frame the debate over worship within the boundaries of style, we will never answer the main question about worship:

What does God desire from our worship?

THE WORSHIP LEADERS MUST WORSHIP

The old joke goes, "How can you tell when a politician is lying?" The answer: "When his lips are moving!"

Jesus Himself said that the Father is looking for true worshippers, who would worship Him in spirit and in truth. Before your church can become a worshipping church, the leaders of the church must first be true worshippers. But you shouldn't take it for granted that those of us on the platform are truly worshipping, just because our lips are moving.

If you are a pastor, music minister, vocalist or band member, you cannot lead your congregation into worship unless you yourself are worshipping God.

Worship leaders are often so caught up in the mechanics of leading worship that having their own worship experience gets pushed to the back burner. As a leader in your congregation, Satan will make it especially hard for you to personally enter into worship. For worship to take place, you must be proactive in preparing your own heart and life to enter the Father's presence. Here's one of the main hindrances to worship many worship leaders face on Sunday…

How's your prayer life?

For you to be a true worshipper, you must cultivate a daily time with God. Perhaps this sounds elementary, but it's easy for all of us to become slack in our own personal worship and prayer with the Lord. While you don't want a "quiet time" to become just a legalistic observance, you can't expect worshipping to come naturally in front of others if it has not been a daily habit done privately before the Lord.

You can't perform on Sunday what you don't practice on Monday.

I've noticed that a congregation will respond to my passion about the Lord as I worship. I can expect for them to reflect about 80% of what I'm willing to give on the platform. As a leader, if you do not have that honest passion, you can either try to fake it or you can lay there like a wet blanket. But neither of those will invite the presence of the Holy Spirit the way honest zeal for God will.

Though you may be able to impress people with musical pyrotechnics, and you may put on the look of worship, the anointing of God will only come when the vessel is pure and passionate. Without the reality of a vibrant daily walk with the Lord, you will be singing about a love that is only a faint memory.

That leads me to my next question…

How honest are you when you are leading worship?

Sincerity and authenticity in worship are musts for the worship leader. True worship is something you cannot fake (though many try). It will be real if you are real and your heart is in tune with God. It will be powerless and fake if your fellowship with God is distant.

I have seen the strangest habits on the platforms of churches across the country. Pastors and music ministers alike adopt affected ways of speaking and gesturing that they believe convey polish and culture. These actually betray a false showmanship and patronizing attitude toward the congregation.

I remember one church where everyone on the platform was instructed to use the phrase, "Please turn your attention to the screens" or "Please turn your attention to the baptistery area" or "Please turn your attention to this week's bulletin". They were not allowed to simply say "Let's all look at the screen".

Tell me, does anybody really talk like that? This kind of artifice cues the congregation that what is happening is scripted and unnatural.

Artifice (that which is artificial) **is the kryptonite of real worship.** While no one wants to look awkward in their worship leading, we must avoid the temptation to choreograph everything we do on the platform. Even when worship is well prepared, it must come from the heart and avoid pretense or performance.

Also, how prepared are you for the "mechanics" of the music?

As much as we'd like people to think that worship happens due to our intense spirituality, there's actually a great deal of practical work beforehand that goes into a weekly service. After you've picked out all the songs and rehearsed all the musicians and vocalists, the amount of personal preparation by the worship leader and pastor can still help determine how smoothly the congregation will be able to enter into worship.

For instance, are their **"speed bumps"** in your worship service? Those are the times when everything stops flowing, and people feel like something is not right. It may be that "pregnant pause" while you are waiting for someone to make his way to the platform. There's that wait while the instrumentalists figure out what song comes next. It may be when the slides on the screen don't match the words you're singing. Or when you move suddenly from a slow song into an uptempo number.

The most well-known cause for worship speed bumps is sound system malfunction, due more to a lack of proper preparation. We probably owe an apology to all the demons we've blamed, when it was really people who are at fault! Whatever the cause, the "speed bumps" break the congregation's concentration upon the Lord, as the worship leader scrambles to fix things. This can cause us to quickly look ridiculous and chaotic.

We guard against this by planning ahead how the songs will flow into each other, telling people to get in place early, and planning all transitions in the service. Do you need to transition into the next song with a short prayer, or a thought that will communicate the song's meaning to the worshipper? Can your pastor's welcome to the congregation be a time for the stage to get reset?

These kinds of concerns may seem petty, but they truly matter. Without planning, we worship leaders can get flustered in the process of worship and miss the blessing that everyone else is receiving.

Finally, **if you're trying to be authentic, what do you do when you're in a bad mood?**

Everybody has bad days: times when you are down, distracted by a family issue, or just plain not feeling good. Since you are the worship leader, you can't always just stay home and curl up on the couch. You can't just phone in and say you're not "feeling it" today. But when you do show up on those days, it's not ok to infect the congregation with your ennui.

Sure, you could simply paste on a happy-face and go out and "sell it" like a trouper. But if worship should be sincere, does that mean that you subject the congregation to your mood of the day?

The correct answer is: "none of the above". Some of the purest praise is done through trials. When God asked us to offer Him the "sacrifice of praise", I think that is referring specifically to these times when worshipping is a struggle. Our lives may be painful at the time, but God is still worthy of our praise. Our hearts may be breaking, but they still belong to Him and were paid for with His blood.

When we are feeling low, that's when it truly is a "sacrifice" for us to praise Him. In spite of our pain, we say, "Praise the Lord, anyhow"!

It means so much to me when I look out at the congregation and see someone who I know may be fighting cancer, yet their voices are lifted in praise just the same. I see someone whose spouse has just left them, but their hands are raised in surrender to the Lord of their destiny. When you see someone who is worshipping amid those circumstances, they are not faking it, they are "faith-ing it". They have made the decision that God is more worthy of their attention than are their problems.

Best of all, when we worship "in spite of it all", we begin to see things from God's point of view instead of their own limited perspective.

Sometimes it's hard to worship freely when people around you are resistant to worship. But when I feel intimidated, I remember the woman with the alabaster box. She had burst into a stranger's home in the middle of their supper. She had taken a prized possession and destroyed it, breaking the alabaster jar to access the perfume inside. She worshipped freely in the midst of opposition, offering something that came at such a great price. While some criticized her worship, Jesus praised her and was blessed by her offering.

That kind of self-sacrificial worship is something I believe delights the Father. Like the perfume in that alabaster jar, our worship in the midst of pain is held deeply precious to him.

    These practical elements of worship, ***prayerful preparation, sincerity of heart, musical preparation, and perseverance in the face of obstacles*** are essential to real worship.

Anything less, and you are just practically worshipping.

INSIDE OUT WORSHIP

It's kind of funny how most everyone considers me a rather jovial person. I'm sure they think my sense of humor comes easily, and that cutting up and being silly are second nature to me.

If they only knew how hard I have to fight for my joy.

My wife knows it. She's watched me battle with seasons of discouragement off and on for years now. I grew up in a family where negativity was the default outlook. And as a creative person, being self-critical is how I've become good at the art I do. But not knowing when to turn that critical searchlight off can make the artist destroy himself.

When I hear how many people today struggle with depression and other mental health issues, I'm amazed at worship services I watch online. They are ignoring the one thing their congregation needs more than anything.

Joy. They all desperately need at least a little joy.

But instead, one service I watched on the internet just the other day went like this:

After the countdown video, moody stage lighting comes up. A wispy young lady dressed in drab tones sang a medium tempo song about no matter how hard things are, God's gonna get us through.

OK, that's a valid message. Not necessarily the one I want to hear right after dropping the kids off in Children's Church and rushing to the sanctuary. But hey, I'm running on fumes just to get to church. Glad I brought a cup of coffee from the lobby. I'll need it.

Now onto the next song, connected to the previous one by a droning synthesizer hum sounding like the underscoring to an 80s slasher film. I halfway expected someone to jump out of the shadows onstage with a knife.

But no, that would have actually been exciting. And nothing is exciting in this service.

This second song is a really slow one. Terrific. Everything it says about God is true, there's nothing wrong with the theology. But it's *how* they sang it. I believe the best word to describe it would be "perfunctory".

It's like they were saying, "Here's what God's like. Whatever."

These beautiful young people onstage, most with less than 15% body fat, never looked happy to be there. In fact, they looked rather non-plussed the whole time. You certainly wouldn't think they were overwhelmed by God's presence.

You'd be stretching it to say they were even just "whelmed".

Thankfully a staff member broke up the monotony to welcome everyone. He wasn't the actual pastor, but a "mini-pastor" who does the stuff the real pastor doesn't want to. In very serious tones, he said "Welcome to our service. We value you here". It sounded like the doctor's office recording saying, "We value your call".

The synthesizer droned on endlessly underneath him.

"Maybe he's the Slasher!", I wondered to myself. No, he's just there to restate once more the church's motto: you know, the one on the screen, and on the bulletin, and on the visitor card, and on the banner as you came in the lobby, and on the billboard on the way to the church, and…

Once the Slasher, …er, um, "mini-pastor" had left the stage, we were treated to one more song…E V E N S L O W E R T H A N T H E L A S T O N E…………. The lighting grew even moodier, if that's possible. All the young, beautiful praise team members hung their under-30-year-old heads, bowed either in prayerfulness or perhaps they had just lost a contact lens…

What in the name of Chris Tomlin is going on with this? Why is it considered "inauthentic" to show positive enthusiasm in God's presence? If one of the characters from Pixar's *Inside Out 2* had led this service, it would have been the mopey "Ennui" girl, with her eyes rolling and head tilted sideways!

Sure, I get that encountering God's Spirit can bring conviction of sin. I'm all for that. But worship when it's most effective takes our thoughts OFF ourselves and ON to the wondrous God we serve! While repentance should be a part of the service, shouldn't joy and praise be part of it as well?

It may all come down to a misunderstanding of what "authentic" worship is.

Some of today's worship seems to be a reaction to the overly "happy clappy" worship of the 80s and 90s. Integrity Music produced a series of worship albums full of energy and peppy choruses, all blending one into the other. Some of those albums probably lacked depth, though you would never accuse that era's prophets like Keith Green of soft-selling anything about the Gospel. However, I get where the pendulum might have needed to swing back the other direction a bit to show a fuller spectrum of worship.

But "authenticity" does not mean looking defeated and singing songs that sound like they all came from the book of Lamentations. It's as if all the "emo" bands of the 90s had kids who grew up to lead worship! If you are that consistently depressive in the presence of God, you need to seek some counseling. Seriously, I'm not joking. That is not a spiritually or emotionally balanced way to function on a church platform.

Some may argue that joyful, high-energy songs fall on deaf ears for people dealing with depression. But as someone who fights with seasons of discouragement, one of the best things a worship service can do is remind me that regardless of what I'm going through, God is good! My circumstances may not be good, but God still is! So joyful worship can take my focus off myself and back onto the God who deserves it.

I need to experience joy when I come to church. And I'll bet everyone else does as well!

All those times we were told in the Bible to "magnify the Lord" in worship meant we were to focus solely on Him. When we bring Him frontmost in our line of sight, we realize how small our problems truly are.

We shouldn't take it lightly when the Bible says, "the joy of the Lord is your strength" (Nehemiah 8:10). If I'm your enemy and want to destroy you, I'll strategically attack your joy. If I can first drain you of hope, I won't have to fight you - you'll give up on your own.

The smartest most strategic thing any worship leader should do every Sunday is, no matter what other songs you do, lead at least one or two songs upfront that speak faith over your congregation. I'm not talking about silly "name it and claim it faith", but faith that stares reality square in the face but trusts a good God is still in control!

A stubborn faith that shines a wide-open smile into the abyss, and uses praise as the weapon of spiritual warfare it was meant to be.

There was a good reason Jehoshaphat put the choir in front of his army as he went into battle. When you want God to fight for you, put down your weapons and your praise out front. And when you want to help your people fight not only this dreary world but their own personal demons, joy is the prescription they need most!

So be authentic, but authentically joyful. Before you head onto the platform to lead, crucify your selfish feelings, get over yourself, and focus on the God who can lift you and your congregation above it all.

And if you're choosing a worship leader again from the characters in *Inside Out 2*, make sure it's always "Joy"!

A WORSHIPPING CHURCH

As a child, I took two allergy shots every week from the age of 6 to 17. I always wondered why I felt a little draggy the day after I took the shot, until I discovered that they were actually injecting me with some of the very stuff that caused my sinuses to flare up. And if you take a flu shot, most times you are receiving a weak strain of that actual flu, so that your body will build up its defenses for when the real thing comes along.

I'm afraid that we've done something similar in the church, but with tragic results. By subjecting church members to years of weak and impotent worship, we've inoculated them against ever catching a real passion for God. After years of enduring services where no one expects God to move, they've begun to think that's the way church is supposed to be. After all, good medicine is supposed to taste bad, right?

I grew up in a Southern Baptist church, and our denomination has always been known for its preaching of the Word of God. However, in all those years growing up, I had never heard a sermon delivered on one of the most important ideas in the Bible…

I never heard one sermon or attended one class on the topic of Biblical worship.

We were told that we were supposed to come to worship services, and that we had better not worship any other gods or we'd be in big trouble. But as to **how** we were supposed to accomplish this worship, or just what God desired in it, we were left totally in the dark. It never occurred to anyone to ask why we were doing this, or rather, for **Whom** we were doing it.

With that in mind, I'd like for you to take a few minutes to give your own church a "checkup". God wants to work through the worship in your church to change lives and draw people into His glorious presence. But He is not allowed to do that at every church. Is He welcomed to move freely at your church?

Is your church "real" or "surreal"?

Authenticity is important for corporate worship to touch the heart of God as well as minister to the congregation. If worship is always uptempo and surface, worshippers will not discover how to worship God in their times of hurt and need. And if worship is always slow and mournful, worshippers will be starved for the "joy of the Lord".

Just as it is important that worship touches the full spectrum of human emotions, you must always guard against worship becoming simply an emotional experience. While I've been frustrated with the dryness of many of the Baptist services I've attended, it is just as pointless to have emotion as an end in itself. When I've seen someone worshipping in a strange manner that is not prescribed in Scripture, I can't help but wonder about their heart-motive. However, emotion is not evil – it is a natural part of the human experience. Therefore, it must be part of the worship experience.

While acknowledging that abuses occur, we still need to be careful about discouraging someone's expressions of worship unless it is truly causing disruption in the church. There are some things that brothers and sisters in Christ do in services that really irritate me. But if I am going to ask them to stop, I need to have good Biblical footing to make that request. If I'm not careful, I can not only hurt someone's feeling, but I may also grieve the Holy Spirit.

If you counsel with someone who you believe is a true distraction to the congregation's worship, you might approach them with a question. You could say, "Is what you are doing calling more attention to the Lord, or to you?" If they are truly sensitive to the Holy Spirit, this may cause the believer to rethink how their worship affects others. Though they may have the "right" to do it, it may not be what is best for the Body as a whole. We need to find a way to give God all the glory He is due, while still respecting the need of others to worship also.

Whatever we do in worship, please be sure we "keep it real". While lack of participation is discouraging, participation forced by a guilt trip is worse. God doesn't need our help by trying to stir up emotions. When God shows up in worship, don't worry…it will be exciting enough without any of our manipulation.

While you want to be well prepared for your service, be careful making things "too perfect". I've seen praise teams that were cued to make a dramatic move to the edge of the stage in unison, usually at a key change or high point of the song. While that kind of thing works well in Vegas, it can make a time of worship look more like a mere performance. The congregation will respond by watching the "show" and not participating. Too much slickness takes away from the authenticity of what God is doing.

Is worship a priority in your church?

Every minister I've ever met would say that worship is an important ingredient in their services. Yet a look at their worship orders may betray a lack of attention given to the practice of worship itself.

Time is taken up for numerous announcements of church activities, those sick in the hospital, and the welcoming of guests. There may also be numerous performance numbers done by soloists or the choir in which the congregation is not encouraged to participate. And don't get me started on endless video bumpers and sermon starters.

I have also known a few pastors whose sermon length does not allow ample time for worship to go on beforehand. When this subject came up once in a conversation, one lady informed me that it was OK because "only the sermon matters anyway". As important as a sermon is to a worship service, a wise pastor desires for true worship to take place before they deliver the Word of God. Their sermon will be much more effective with a powerful worship set behind it.

But remember, the sermon is really for you, not God. The worship is the thing we do to bless the heart of God. So when you neglect the worship, you're just being selfish. You're neglecting to ask what God wants from your service.

What are the things in your service that take up time that could be used worshipping the Father? As much as we want to meet the needs of people, our first priority must be blessing the Lord, not placating the people. We need to prioritize time for worship, so that God's Spirit is allowed to move and work among His people.

Does the music encourage the congregation to participate?

If your people are predominantly rural folks, you probably need to pick a style of music that they can relate to easily (maybe throw in some Southern Gospel and hymns). If they are young urbanites, something with a contemporary edge would probably be better. But if the congregation has trouble relating to the style of music, it will be hard for them to get to a place where their attention moves away from the music and onto the Lord. And while variety does keep things interesting, you need to find a "median style" and hover around it with occasional exceptions.

Regardless of the style you pick, singing with passion and conviction is what makes the difference. I saw one church's service on TV recently that was trying to update their music. As I watched their "new & improved" service, they were singing modern praise choruses… but sang them with the same lack of enthusiasm they gave the old hymns before. This is not progress!

It doesn't matter so much what style of music you sing as **how you sing it!** You can drain the life out of just about any piece of music if you sing with apathy. But you'd be surprised how people will respond to different styles of music when the song is simply sung with passion.

Is there a flow to your service outline?

In looking at a diagram for the Temple from the Old Testament, we can see an outline for how we enter into worship. The Bible says to "enter His gates with Thanksgiving" and "His courts with praise", which would seem to suggest a logical progression. So I start my services with more uptempo, "lighter" worship songs to get the congregation moved through the "front gates" of worship. As we move farther into the presence of the Lord, the music gradually becomes more and more intense and passionate. Hopefully, we end up in His presence at the Holy of Holies.

I think God set it up this way because He understands people. We don't always walk into a worship service feeling spiritual. It takes us a while to shake off the "spirit of heaviness" form the world and put on the "garment of praise". In the opening worship set, I try to grab their attention and put it on what the Lord has done for them personally. As the service progresses, we focus more on worshipping God for who He is than for what He has given us or done for us. Hopefully, by the time the Pastor gets up to deliver the message from God's Word, we have a clear picture of who God is and have invited His presence into the service.

Grouping songs based on tempo as well as theme may help, as well as transitioning between songs without jarring stops and restarts. You may need to speak of few words of prayer to transition and focus the worshippers on the direction you are heading. The goal is to make things move from one element to the other with as much grace as possible.

Is the atmosphere conducive to worship?

As we get into a more intense and intimate time of worship, I will often ask that the house lights be lowered. I'm not doing this so that the service seems more like a performance. I've found some people (especially men) worship better if they feel no one is looking at them. Lowering the house lights takes away some of the congregation's self-consciousness and allows them to more freely focus on the Lord.

Here again, you want to be careful about getting carried away with too much affected lighting. While special lighting effects are a big part of a pop music concert, they can give worship an artificial feel. I try to avoid any lighting effects that call attention to themselves. The more subtle the better. Make any changes in lighting with as little fanfare as possible.

Does the sound constantly distract from your service? Today's sound boards are not meant to be operated by just any volunteer. Also, just because someone understands electronics doesn't mean they have an ear for mixing instrumentation and vocals. The people who come to our churches today are used to digital quality sound. If your church budget can stand it, I'd suggest hiring a professional who will run the system for Sunday services.

Do the people on the platform blend in or stand out from the worship? While you never want church to become a beauty pageant, people on the praise team or in the choir need to be encouraged to look their very best...whatever that is. I personally am happy men can now feel free to untuck their shirts, as I've often felt my midsection could become a negative focal point in worship. Likewise, we don't need to try to look sexy or provocative.

Do you allow time for God to change lives?

If everything in your service is over-programmed, you may be guilty of not leaving time for the Holy Spirit to work in people's lives. While planning the sermon and preparing the music are important, the most important work in hearts is done not by our efforts but by the Spirit of God. You need to allow time for God to work and move among your people, and not just speed from song to song to sermon.

I've often had a time of prayer at the altar as the worship begins to be more passionate. We ask those who have a need to move to the altar area and lay their burdens before the Lord. Other people flow forward to pray with them, placing a hand on their shoulders. We will usually repeat some gentle praise chorus in the background while this is happening, so worship can continue for those who may not be praying.

Having a specific time of prayer at the altar allows another way for people to be involved in worship and not just observe it. It ministers in a special way to those currently enduring a struggle or spiritual trial.

Does God leave your service honored by the worship?

In worship, the goal is not to entertain the congregation, but to be a personal blessing to the Lord himself. Just think of it… there are few things you can do that are a direct blessing to the Lord. We all know that you can benefit His church through acts of service, tithes and offerings. But in worship, you are actually ministering directly to God. That is nothing short of the highest and holiest calling I can imagine!

And if you look to the Bible, you will see that God gives very specific ingredients that He expects to be present in worship. Cain's worship was not acceptable to God because He didn't offer a blood sacrifice as God prescribed, but instead offered the fruit of his own crops. This was Cain's preference in worship, and it was much more convenient for him than going and getting an animal to sacrifice.

But just as Cain's convenience and comfort were not the issue, so our preferences are no excuse for not being a blessing to the Father in worship.

Churchgoers every Sunday are substituting their own preferences in worship for what God desires. If we are uncomfortable with singing in worship, we just refuse to sing. If we grew up with no clapping in services, we simply refrain from clapping. And if we think that lifting our hands in praise might lead someone to look at us oddly, we worship with our hands conveniently at our sides.

But God has let us know through His Word what He wants from our worship. And if worship is really about God's desires and not ours, perhaps we should learn to be better hosts and hostesses to Him on Sunday!

The question that most churches today are asking is, "How do we make people more comfortable in our services?" But what they should be asking is, "How do we make GOD more welcomed by our worship?"

We have bought the lie that we can worship God any way we want to. You might want to ask King David and Uzzah about how that idea worked for them in 2 Samuel, chapter 6. It was more convenient for them to move the Ark of the Covenant with an ox cart than to go to the trouble of doing it the way God had prescribed. But when Uzzah fell over dead while touching the Ark (against the rules), David suddenly realized the hard way that worship was not about his preference, nor his convenience.

Worship is about hosting our very Special Guest. To be a good host, we must go to great lengths to give the Guest what He wants…even at the expense of what we desire.

Many of us might be ashamed to admit the true state of our church's worship. But admitting our neediness before God is the first step toward repentance from dry-eyed, passionless worship. By humbling ourselves before Him and putting God first, we put ourselves in the position for Him to revive us and resurrect our worship!

SACRED COWS & CAMEL TIPPING

There's a rule called "Chesterton's Fence", which is meant as a caution to people hoping to change an institution for the better. Author G.K Chesterton warned you should never destroy a fence (as in changing a rule or cancelling a tradition) until you know why it was in place in the first place. If not, you may inadvertently saw off the very tree limb on which you're sitting.

I've learned through the years that it may not just be a fence in your way. Sometimes it's a camel.

On YouTube, there is a video of a camel falling into a crowd of people during a church Christmas production. It is both hilarious and terrifying to watch, as the huge beast stumbles and sits down on a section of pews. Thankfully, the crowd moved out of the way quickly and no one was hurt, including "Lula Bell" the camel.

I'll wait while you Google it…

What makes this video special to me is that I once served that very church and led that very Christmas program. No, this didn't happen when I was there. I actually said no to the camel for my productions, but it was later reinstated after I left.

Nevertheless, that camel taught me a lesson or two.

I served for two years as the music minister for that church where their big tradition was a huge annual Christmas spectacular. They hired a 25-piece orchestra and had professional arrangers orchestrating music just for them. They made tons of costumes and had an actualy Broadway set designer for their set. They brought in professional lighting designers, and rented state-of-the-art lights that would have made most rock concerts envious. The whole thing cost nearly $200,000, and they charged people who attended the 11 yearly performances.

You might be thinking $200,000 is more than the entire budgets for some churches, and you'd be right. You also may remember that time when Jesus tipped the money tables over in the temple. So you might be wondering how Jesus would feel about charging people to enter a church.

That's a pretty good question. We'll come back to that later…

As the new guy they'd just hired, I naturally wanted to make some changes. There were several things about the production I thought could be better.

For one thing, they did about an hour and a half of secular Christmas music but spent only 30 to 40 minutes on the life of Christ. That's right, they boiled down everything from the Nativity to the Ascension into the time of a TV sitcom.

Though I like "Jingle Bells" as much as the next guy, I immediately switched the emphasis. The secular program would go down to around 45 minutes, and the Life of Christ section would expand to around 75 minutes.

My next problem was Jesus. Not the actual Jesus, but the guy who played our "Jesus". Through no fault of his own, he was getting old. And quite bald. Sure, his hair was still long, but he was balding on top. He looked a bit like Riff Raff from Rocky Horror Picture Show. But instead of asking him to step down, year after year they keep letting him play the part.

When I handed my script out to the cast, the eyes of "Old Jesus" glazed over. Why? In my script, Jesus actually spoke words straight from Scripture. But "Old Jesus" had only stood onstage with his arms outstretched and hugged the occasional child like a politician. Soon, "Old Jesus" bowed out and we cast a young college actor who actually looked Jewish. I was thrilled.

In the midst of all these major revisions to the program, there was one more minor change I wanted to make. And that one probably was my death sentence. I nixed the camel coming down the aisle for the big Nativity scene.

My thinking was two-fold. First, the camel was a huge expense. Probably $10,000 to $15,000 would end up being spent to rent and house a camel on our property for the 2 to 3 weeks of our show. That seemed like a ridiculous amount of money for one animal.

Second, camels are disgusting, mercurial creatures that can get moody very quickly. She would be lead down an aisle surrounded by pews filled with people. The camel could get spooked by all the flashing lights and the noise of a hundred-voice choir plus orchestra. A child could easily dart out into the aisle and be trampled. With all of these factors weighed together, along with the lingering smell of poop we'd have in the sanctuary for weeks, I told the crew we'd be skipping the camel this year.

Switching Jesuses was one thing. But messing with the camel was literally "the last straw".

People hated me. No, REALLY hated me. I was not only the new upstart Music Minister who'd replaced the guy who retired after 30+ years. Now I was the Grinch who stole the Christmas camel! And this time, the Whos in Whoville were not holding hands and singing.

They were cursing the day I'd ever darkened their $200,000 doors.

I made it about another year and a half at that church before both they and I had finally had enough of each other. But I learned several lessons there that have stuck with me through the years.

One is found in the wisdom of Proverbs 22:28:

"Remove not the ancient landmark, which thy fathers have set."

In other words, don't tear down "Chesterton's fence" until you know why it's there. Though all my changes were well-intentioned, I would have been wise to shift things more incrementally over time. All those changes in one year were too much for a church to swallow. It didn't matter that they were the right changes. The rapidity of the changes made them intolerable for the people, no matter how right I may have been.

Another lesson was how a church can rationalize irrational expenses, if they want to. My church defended the exorbitant costs by saying the show brought people to Christ. We drew them in with the entertaining spectacle, and then slipped in the message of the Gospel. As many of the production's defenders would say to me, "If even one person comes to faith in Christ as a result, it was worth every penny!"

But here's the funny thing about that. After the production was over, I did an audit of the spiritual results. I looked at the commitment cards people filled. I also checked to see how many of those people had actually become members of our church or been baptized as a result of our program.

Zero. Not one person. In the two years I did that overblown production, my personal Captain Ahab experience, I could not verify one person who started living for Jesus and joined our church as a result. And that was AFTER refocusing the content on Jesus.

Hmmm. Maybe it was because the camel stayed home?

Jesus found it problematic when the priests at the temple mixed their own selfish motives with the temple worship. They started a racket where they rejected the animal sacrifices people brought and then sold them new animals at a much greater cost. They said they were just helping people's sacrifices be acceptable to God. But what they were really doing was making a fast buck, and that's what ticked Jesus off. It wasn't that money changed hands in church, it was that people had to endure extortion to worship in God's House.

That's a picture of just how easy it is to mix your own selfish motives with God's. Don't be so hard on them, since we all have our own expensive "camels" we're rationalizing.

Most of the greatest pastors I've known look like failures next to the guys with the multimillion dollar budgets and huge congregations. Lots of pastors become successful by giving people all the Christmas camels they want. But the hand of God will not be in it if the voice of God never initiated it. We run the risk of being yet another Sisyphus, rolling our dumb rocks up a hill only to watch them roll back down on us in the end.

Or maybe a better analogy would be a camel toppling over on us. Like in that video taken a few years after I left that church and they put everything back the way they wanted it. I have to say it felt like sublime payback when I saw "Lula Bell" tip over on YouTube. By the grace of God, no one was hurt.

In fact, in my own twisted mind, I've wondered: could it have been Jesus who tipped the camel, just to make a point like He did in the Temple 2000 years prior?

"Surely, Jesus wouldn't do anything that outrageous", you say. But to predict future events, it's always best to observe past performance.

And whether it's money tables or camels, we're smart to stay out of Jesus' way and do what He wants instead.

DIVINE MISTAKES

To correct the problem of church announcements taking time away from worship, churches have begun programming their services more carefully. Each song, every announcement, often each transitional word spoken is prescribed ahead of time. It's true that you must have a plan. I'm not for just showing up unprepared and waiting to see what happens.

But many churches today are perilously close to programming the Holy Spirit out of their services. If God's Spirit never showed up, would your service happen anyway, just as planned.

Just like with our daily lives, we all want worship to go smoothly. We beg God to stay with our plan and keep to our schedule. But sometimes God wants our plans to fall apart so His plan can go into action.

When I lead a worship service, I plan every detail out specifically. I respect people's time, so I try to be prepared for any eventuality. But despite my best efforts, I vividly remember one Sunday at my church that was a train wreck. It started off bad, and then steam rolled out of control as the service progressed.

To begin with, I was running late that morning. When we arrived to set up at the middle school we rented each Sunday, we noticed the media cart with the connections to the auditorium's video projector was missing. Gone. Nowhere to be found.

Without it, it would be impossible to project the songs we picked out onto our video screen and throw a huge monkey-wrench in my worship plan. But this just served as an opportunity to send my incredible volunteers into action. These resourceful men found a way to attach a patch cord directly into the projector that was mounted in the auditorium's ceiling. It would have to hang down awkwardly in the center of the front row, but it was certainly better than no video at all. What a team!

As we got into the worship music of the service, some sound system problems caused the music to suddenly boost to an uncomfortable level. When I turned my wireless mic on later at the start of the sermon, feedback filled the room. But that was not the worst crisis to befall me that morning…

My hair gel failed.

To any other pastor, this would be a minor irritation if not left completely unnoticed. But I have really big hair. And only large helpings of hair gel will keep it all in place.

We ship it to my home on trucks, in large, industrial-sized containers. I'm only slightly kidding.

As I'm preaching, my hair begins to fall in my face. Now I'm continually running my fingers through it, trying to get it to stay up on my head. Fail. Trying again. Failing again.

Then, my cell phone gives off a little "notification ring". I laugh to the congregation, "Oh, who would be texting the pastor during his sermon?" I pick it up to read a text from my wife in front of the whole congregation.

"Stop messing with your hair. It looks fine."

The room explodes with laughter.

Then just as I'm getting toward the big conclusion of the message, THE POWER GOES OUT!

You may think this service sounds like one huge disaster, but in the end it was quite the opposite. When I finished the message and gave an invitation, we saw several people come forward to respond to God's Word. In fact, God answered some prayers that day I had been praying for over a year. Wow.

If you think it's impossible for God to work through a train wreck like what I've described, then I have a message for you...

Dear Control Freak: just stop it already. Right now. Seriously.

You know who you are. You're the ones who must have everything done "just so". You call it being "organized and thorough", but in truth you're really just a control freak. And if you don't get your controlling under God's control soon, you're going to program God out of your service and miss some of His best blessings for your life!

I've watched control freaks for years ruining the lives of their friends and family. They are the ones at holiday gatherings expecting everything to go perfectly, despite having a roomful of divergent personalities and opinions. They demand their employees not only get the job done but do it exactly the way they would do it.

They are also the parents shaming their overweight kids, just because they want them to be "healthy". And we see them all over social media right now finding racism in every statement and in every heart. They feel they must right every wrong, and everyone but them are the ones in the wrong.

Take it from me, your tweaks are as welcomed as being pecked to death by a duck.

The sad part is that whether you're right or you're wrong, what you're doing is not going to work. Why? Because eventually people will get tired of being dominated by you. I've also noticed that human nature works against controlling people. After a while, most people double-down on the very behavior you're trying to change.

The worst part is when controlling habits creep into your spiritual life. A.W. Tozer once said, "When we come to the place where everything [in the worship service] can be predicted, and nobody expects anything unusual from God, we are in a rut."

The same is true for your life. You think you're being responsible and cautious. But really you're just a coward. As a result, your life becomes dull and predictable. However, it is also peaceful.

Peaceful like a graveyard.

I love what the famous art teacher and TV personality Bob Rose said whenever he made a mistake painting:

"We don't make mistakes, we make happy accidents"

In the same way, film director Orson Welles talked about the importance of going with the flow in his technique. Far from trying to control every detail, he once explained:

> *"the greatest things in movies are divine accidents… my definition of a film director is the man who presides over accidents… everywhere there are beautiful accidents… they're the only things that keep a film from being dead"*

But when we try to take too much control, we leave little room for God to do His best work. In the end, we get only what we can accomplish with our own limited skills and insight. What a waste!

Coincidently, the sermon on that "trainwreck Sunday" was on when Jesus prodded Peter to walk on water with Him. I was encouraging people to allow Jesus to make their lives an adventure, to "walking on water", taking risks, and live in the moment. And what God had just done is illustrate my sermon better than any pastor could ever expect!

I imagine if Peter hadn't stepped out of the boat that night around 3am with Jesus, there would not have been another opportunity. He saw his opening, he asked Jesus if it was OK, then he just stepped out into the Sea of Galilee. He didn't wait for good conditions. In fact, the conditions were the worst possible for water walking – a storm. Yet he took hold of the opportunity in the midst of an imperfect situation and became one of only two people to ever be held upright by nothing but H2O.

I want to live a life like that – something that's worth telling my grandkids about one day. How I stepped out on a crazy whim and went on an adventure with Jesus. And together, we changed the world! Well, mostly Him…but I helped.

That Sunday morning, our service certainly was a train wreck. But I went with the flow and had one of my best preaching experiences ever. Lives were changed and I left invigorated and inspired. The best parts of it were completely unplanned, spontaneous, and out-of-control. It was something only God could have done…through me.

This is the life Jesus is calling you to – a messy, random, magical existence. An unpredictable comedy of errors you could never plan in a million years. A story too unlikely and amazing to be believed. And yet it is happening right before your eyes.

So while you work diligently to remove all the "speed bumps' from your service and seek to glorify God with your music, remember to do this as well…

Stop over-planning. Stop worrying. Embrace the chaos. Enjoy the ride.

Then tell your grandkids.

"I SEE DEAD PEOPLE"

Where are you most likely to hear the phrase "I see dead people"?

1. *In the movie "The Sixth Sense"*
2. *The cemetery*
3. *Spoken under the worship leader's breath during the early service*

"Ha…good one!" you say.

But seriously folks, it's no joke.

One of the services I lead each Sunday at my church starts at 8AM. My job may not look too hard, but I challenge you to get people to sing along with you, not to mention getting them to actually "worship" at such an hour. It won't be long before you understand why the Lord had to tell Jeremiah "Don't be afraid of their faces"!

Because getting people to respond is such an uphill battle, many worship leaders have stopped trying. They settle for letting the congregation just be an audience, and they do all the "performing" themselves. While I understand their frustration, they've turned themselves into little more than "Christian entertainers".

In turn, our congregations often come to church today to "see the show". The trend in some of our most respected churches is for the congregation to feel no need to participate. I've noticed some of these churches consider themselves to be on the cutting edge in worship due to their use of lighting and technology. They believe they've come a long way from their grandparents' church, with their antiquated hymns and organ music.

But what they've really done is trade worship with hymns that no one was singing for worship with choruses that still no one is singing. That's not progress.

It's a bit like the movie *Weekend at Bernie's*. We think if we just move the corpse around enough, it will convince people it's alive. But when God's desire is participation from His people, dead contemporary worship is no better than dead old-fashioned worship. Use all the moving lights and smoke you like, but like Bernie, that's still a corpse no matter how you dress him up!

The church today reminds me a lot of Lazarus from the Bible, in how desperately we need Jesus to raise us from the dead. The problem with worship in many of our churches is a spiritual one. So like the messenger who came to Jesus, it's about time we admit the true condition of the church today...

"The one you love is sick..."

When someone you love is sick, nothing else matters. That's just how Mary and Martha felt when they sent word to Jesus that their brother Lazarus was dying. They expected Jesus to drop everything, especially since He was a personal friend. But Jesus waited before He came, because He wanted us to learn something about responding in the midst of a crisis.

He wanted us to know that He is still in control.

But what if the one who is sick is not a friend – it's your church? Over the years you've watched as members have left, needs have gone unmet, and morale has drained from the one you love. Now you look into the spiritual eyes of this beloved church and you can see the signs of one struggling with a life-threatening illness.

If this sounds like your church, you've got lots of company. The average church today is sick…in some cases, critically ill. As I talk with ministers from around the country, their problems are so strikingly similar it is alarming.

Our churches, and often our pastors, have bought the lie that worship is about us. We are the consumers, the pastors are the salesmen, and God is some kind of spiritual Costco we visit for free samples each Sunday. Instead of sacrificing our preferences about worship, we take up offense whenever we are not sufficiently stroked, pampered, or pleased. The Bride of Christ is often more reminiscent of the "Bride of Frankenstein", shrieking and hissing her disapproval of any offering we may lay at her feet.

Likewise, our pastors and ministers are often the "Jekyll and Hydes" of the Church. We gripe about the demands of our people, yet we cater to them like fussy waiters in a French restaurant. While we endlessly compare ourselves to another fellowship down the street or across the state, we forget that God has a specific place and a call for our church…if we would only really seek Him for it!

When God is taken off of a church's throne of worship, it throws everything off about that church. Nothing functions properly when the main thing is out of place. And God and His desires are what's missing from most local fellowships. We are on the throne and determined to stay there with our preferences and demands.

The common missing ingredient is the power of God working through His church. When someone is sick, their physical vitality is impeded. Likewise, the Church's spiritual vitality is impeded by the absence of God's power working through the Body of Christ. And that absence is largely due to our impotent worship.

However, many of the dying churches I have observed would refuse the medicine for their disease because, for them, the cure seems worse than the sickness. Churches die because they won't embrace God's agenda. They blame their ineffectiveness on their changing neighborhood, or the lack of talented staff, or what some other church is doing.

But if the gates of Hell can't stand against God's Church, how could these pitiful little foes do any great damage? God wants to do something great in every church, but it is up to that church to follow His lead. And it is by a lack of courage and faith that the equation breaks down.

Is the power of God working freely in your church? Ask yourself the following questions:

Do you regularly see lives transformed by the power of the Gospel?

Do you ask God to work the miraculous, healing lives, putting marriages back together, changing the community around you?

If not, then your church is at least sick, possibly even dead. And the sooner you acknowledge that fact, the quicker God can step in to resurrect it.

"If he sleeps, he'll be better"

Jesus' thoughtful response that Lazarus was merely asleep was completely lost on the disciples. In spite of the level of desperation around them, they concluded that Jesus' sensitivity in phrasing meant that Lazarus had nodded off and would wake up soon. Finally, Jesus has to bluntly state, "He's dead." Death is painful enough, without having a group of dense onlookers hanging around wondering what all the fuss is about.

Ever been to a dead mall? It's a pretty sad place. We used to live in a town that went out on a limb and built a big mall to compete with shopping in the neighboring big city. At first all the hoopla, bells, and whistles attracted some of the curious. But one by one, store after store folded or defected. Within five years, all that was left was a bunch of empty store windows and a parade of senior adults in jogging suits marching through to get a little exercise before the all-you-can-eat buffet.

That's a good picture of so many of the churches we all grew up in. They became focused on their past or in pleasing some constituency within the body. And today, those churches are ghost towns – a shell of what they once were.

And what about worship? In spite of the revival of worship in the last 2 decades, many churches still cling to what is comfortable and easily sustainable, thinking that truly encountering God in worship is another fad that will soon pass away. They have not discovered what the true purpose of worship is, while God is moving elsewhere, doing a great work. Like the Pharisees who prayed inside the Temple for the Messiah to come as Jesus rode past on a donkey outside, God's activity is right under their noses… and yet they miss it entirely!

The plot of *"Weekend at Bernie's"* was that two guys happened upon a mobster right after he had died, and in order to keep from getting killed themselves they make it look like "Bernie" is still alive and kicking. While this sounds unrealistic, it shouldn't to those trapped in a dead or dying church. I've been there, and there's nothing funny about it.

It's frustrating when no one else is willing to admit the prognosis is terminal. Sometimes the denial is because of pride. People don't like to admit that "their team" is losing, and pastors and staff will go to tremendous lengths to prop up the corpse of their own creation. They will often point to a bevy of activities as a sign of health. They point out the numbers of people that still may attend their church.

While programs, people, and prestige aren't inherently bad things, they are not evidence of true spiritual health. Just as our friends in the movie could manipulate Bernie's lifeless corpse to do many lifelike movements, activities can give a church the illusion of life. We can flap her arms around and insist the church is alive and kicking, while playing the part of a spiritual ghoul. We can even dress her up in expensive trappings to make her look important, but to no avail.

Without God's power in worship, we are simply propping up rotting flesh that is most often the creation of our own flesh in its lust for success. We have become spiritual Dr. Frankensteins, trying to desperately zap life back into something that has become a grotesque abomination of real life. We may be able to fool a few easily impressed people, but we are not fooling God.

"If you had been here, He wouldn't have died"

According to Lifeway research published in 2023, there were more church closures than church starts in 2019. And that was BEFORE the Covid pandemic. Now that rate is increasing even more rapidly. It's so easy to assign blame as to why our church is dying, because that way we avoid taking our own responsibility for what has happened.

Just as Lazarus' sisters blamed Jesus for their brother's death, we need someone to pin the blame on when we discover that our church is terminal. Can you sense the irony as Mary and Martha are scolding "The Lord of Heaven and Earth" for His tardiness? And if they trusted Him to heal their brother, why couldn't they now believe that Jesus could raise their brother from the dead? Their bottom line was that they wanted Jesus to do it "their way", and now they were ticked that He had another plan.

Churches members love to blame their pastors for the church's problems. Numerous pastors are fired each year simply because members feel they need "a change in leadership", never dreaming that the real problem could be the member's lack of "followship". I believe God will hold churches accountable for the Godly men they have discarded like yesterday's trash, and some churches now deal with God's discipline because of how they have treated their ministers. The families of ministers that have been uprooted and damaged irrevocably is a disgrace and horrible witness of the love and unity we are supposed to possess in Christ.

Regardless of whose fault it is, we have access to a Power that can overcome our weaknesses and mistakes. However, we must be willing for God to do it "His way". He may not do it on our timetable, and our preaching or innovative methods may not get the credit for it if He steps in. We must allow Him to work as He wishes, and then give Him all the credit when the fire falls in the midst of our worship.

"Where have you laid him?"

In which tomb is your church's worship buried? Is it the "denominational" tomb that says "we just don't worship very demonstrably? Or is it the "contemporary" tomb that has sacrificed every part of the church's worship ministry on the altar of what looks hip? With either one, it is a church whose worship has been wrapped in grave cloths and sealed in a vault of spiritual deadness!

We have allowed our people to live in ignorance of what God desires from our worship and have told them they can worship however they like. We have allowed them to sit on the sidelines and not participate actively in the action of worship. We have constructed special services for them to hide from what God is doing today and slip back into the past. Or have we allowed trends to dictate style to the point that the worship leader is a sanctified MC, only allowed to play the very latest Christian hits?

God is doing something amazing in worship today, all over the world! There is no denying it. And it is not about a style of music: style is peripheral. There are dynamic worshipping churches today that reflect every possible musical taste, from liturgical to contemporary. While it is not about style, it is about "passion". But church leaders have too often allowed fear to restrict us from entering into the presence of a living and dynamic God. Our fear may be that passionate worship looks too charismatic, and we don't want to give people the idea we are religious fanatics.

We may be afraid of alienating senior adults (who are often our monetary base), even though we don't have the same fear of alienating younger adults (who are often not our strongest tithers). While we may have tried to play it smart and take the "path of least resistance", that path has rarely led to the foot of the cross.

The tomb of tradition is an easy place to hide. Living there may seem respectful of the past. And a tomb is a comfortable and quiet place for the dead to rest in peace, but it is nowhere for the church of the living God! It will still reek of death, no matter how comfortable and familiar the tomb may be.

"Take away the stone"

In Jesus' day, they put a stone over the tomb to cover up the reality of the decay taking place inside the tomb. You notice that when Jesus commanded them to remove the stone, some people objected. They said that removing the stone would release the stench inside the tomb. But if the stone had never been rolled back, God's miraculous power might never have been revealed.

Reality is a hard thing for congregations to face, and some just "can't handle the truth". So many churches are institutions built on illusions, with layer upon layer of denial built up like years of floor wax. Instead of dealing with the dirt, it's easier for them to just slap another coat of wax over the problem.

I believe God wants us to ask Him to resurrect our churches. The challenge is just too big for our strategies and preferences. However, we must roll the stone away and face reality. You see, Jesus could have just commanded the stone to move by Himself and it would have to obey. But Jesus wants His people to have ownership in the process of God's work! Denying the problems or the sins that are hidden will obstruct the free flow of worship from sweeping through a body of believers. Jesus will not do this part for you.

Take off the grave clothes and burn them

After Jesus called forth Lazarus from the tomb, he instructed those around him to take off his grave clothes. These would have been bandages of cloth wrapped around him, with much the same look as a mummy. Just as it was important to take these filthy bandages off the resurrected Lazarus, it is important that you remove the grave clothes from your church so that worship can be free and unhindered!

If I were sitting with you right now in your church's sanctuary and asked, "What are the things that bind your church from worshipping God freely", what would you say? Would you point to an attitude in your congregation, or a habit of doing things? It may be your allegiance to a tradition created by men and not God that, while not evil in itself, is hampering a new thing that God wishes to do in worship to revitalize your services. And don't ignore the fact that it may be some unconfessed sin among your people or leadership.

Don't worry about the things you cannot change, but ask yourself, "What are the parts of the problem that my attitude or influence affect?" Once God has pointed out those things to you, you must **burn the grave clothes that bound you.** You must cleanse your own heart from the things that have bound your own personal worship, as well as the worship of your congregation.

Just because your fellowship receives some momentary "mercy drops" of blessing does not mean that the resurrection is permanent. As we have learned in our own pilgrimage with the Lord, even though God has made us a new creation in Christ we still will try to revert back to the ways of the "old man".

It is no different with a church. The grave clothes, the things that kept you bound in worship, must be cleansed completely or worship will not be allowed to blossom and flourish. Slowly, the church will slip back into the old diseased ways of their dead flesh.

There are some churches I've known who simply need some old fashioned repentance. Leaders need to acknowledge when they've bowed to the whims of the congregation and ignored the wind of God's Spirit. When they've followed trends and influencers and not the Holy Spirit. Without repenting from those dead works, the rot will continue to infect the church and inhibit healthy growth.

Whatever those grave clothes are that keep your church bound from worship, you must destroy them so that the church cannot revert back to their old dead ways. Don't presume that they will take care of themselves. You must act quickly to protect the work that God has begun in your fellowship, so that the disease infesting those grave clothes will not start to spread once again and destroy the life your fellowship now possesses!

"Then many…believed in Him"

As you can imagine, the news of Lazarus' resurrection spread quickly, gathering quite a crowd around them. People couldn't help but break out in a dead run so they could see the miracle that had taken place. And they especially wanted to see the One who had called forth a man from 3 days in the tomb! Once word got out, nobody had to beg people to come and confirm the miracle… you couldn't keep the people away!

What hoops does your church have to jump through just to get a good crowd there on Sunday morning? Do you give things away, or have a special music artist in? There's nothing wrong with special events, but when the power of God shows up in a church and lives start getting changed, outreach events become obsolete! The worship service itself becomes the attraction, and God is the only special guest you need to invite. And passionate worship is the way we put out the red carpet to show the Holy Spirit He is welcomed!

This may sound like a lot of hype if you've never seen it happen, but there is nothing that can compare with God's hand upon a service working freely. And if we will come out of our denial, if we stop playing the blame game, if we have the faith enough to face the truth about our church, and ourselves, and if we'll purify the place of worship, then we will see the power of God working actively in our resurrected churches.

That's what God is ready to do… if we are ready to be resurrected.

THE OLD RAZZLE DAZZLE

"How can they see with sequins in their eyes?"
Kander & Ebb

Have you noticed some of the gimmicks people use in church worship? You start to see the same things popping up in everyone's worship set. Things like these:

- *candles*

- *choruses with no more than 4 chords*

- *more candles*

- *choruses that all sound like U2 songs (with 4 chords)*

- *video bumpers for every sermon series*

- *the exposed back of an old spinet piano, with a keyboard hidden inside*

- Artsy light bulb ropes dangling from the ceiling

- wax stains on carpet (from too many candles)

There's certainly nothing wrong with trying some new things in worship. God is creative, so His people should be too. However, we want to be careful putting too much faith in worship fad. We should be careful putting too much time and money in them as well.

I'll bet there are two churches nearby that you keep hearing about. They are the talk of the town, but for two different reasons. However, they share a mutual problem of the heart.

Church #1 – The Performance Church

The order of worship he planned was a work of perfection. The service had one topical thread weaving its message through every hymn, chorus, and special musical selection. This same topic was, of course, the same topic touched on in the Pastor's sermon that Sunday.

In addition, the worship leader had chosen just the right number of hymns and choruses to make sure his musically diverse congregation would all be catered to properly. He had organized the songs so well that even the keys the songs were in led seamlessly from one into the other. There were no awkward stops and restarts, no sudden leaps of tempo; all was smooth sailing this morning.

Not only was the service planned perfectly, but also the people performing it were just the "right people". Finally, he had succeeded in getting the old lady with the blue hair and no sense of tempo to retire from her perch on the organ. The hard-of-hearing man on the soundboard, who had the same lightening response time as a government bureaucrat, was finally replaced by a paid soundman. Everyone in the choir was well-dressed and rehearsed.

All of the young, beautiful people poised out front on the praise team had their music memorized. They all were well coiffed, slicked down, and dressed to the hilt in jewel-tone colors. Today the worship leader would reach a new vista in his ministry. Today he would move the ministry to "the next level", and God in heaven would finally be pleased with their worship after years of putting His fingers in His celestial ears!

What I have just described is some worship leaders' idea of "the ultimate" that a worship experience could be: ***perfect performance***. They believe if their pastor only gave them the sermon topics in enough time to prepare, and if they only had better performers, and if they only had better equipment, they would then be able to do a service pleasing to God. It also tacitly implies that without any of these ingredients, it is virtually impossible to achieve anything of value.

Hopefully one day, this worship leader will be at "the right church". That's the one with enough money and enough people to make his, er um, I mean "God's dream" come true.

Notice that nowhere in that worship leader's process did it mention that he had received this "most excellent order of service" as the result of a time of prayer and submission to the Holy Spirit. The service was simply a "fill in the blanks" exercise that fit the topic the Pastor chose for that Sunday. The balance of hymns to choruses was based more on a quota system that was calculated to satisfy the desires of the congregation.

Our friend also betrays his view of ministry as being more about using people (or perhaps misusing them) than using their gifts. In his view, people with inferior gifts are impediments to effective ministry and need to be removed as soon as possible. There is little regard for whether God might use their gifts better in another area of ministry, or whether God has truly called them to the position in which they currently serve.

All that matters to our worship leader is that the people in his ministry perform well and look good. How God is working in their lives, and whether their hearts are holy and humble is not even an issue to him.

THE PURSUIT OF EXCELLENCE

"But," he would respond, "God deserves the very best we can give Him, doesn't He?" After all, King David himself said "I will not give God that which costs me nothing."

Yes, God does expect and deserve our best in worship. Just for the record, I am a classically trained pianist & vocalist. Musical excellence matters to me.

But in worship, our "best" shouldn't be our "best performance" but our "best offering" to God. The best that we can give God is worship that comes from a thankful, sincere heart! Do we really think that the Creator of the universe is impressed with our rendition of some song or hymn? Our performance is nothing compared to what God is listening to in heaven right now.

However, because we are His beloved children, He raises His hand to hush all of heaven's choirs when we worship. Our music compared to heaven's is like a preschool choir compared to a symphony orchestra! But it is because **His Child** is singing that it is special to the Lord. Like any loving father, He loves the sound of His child singing about "how much they love their Daddy"!

Church #2: The Pageant Church

Churches often focus all their energies on a big theatrical production, such as an Easter or Christmas pageant. The problem becomes people will focus on the spectacle of the performance and lose sight of worship. Then the pressure comes to make the production bigger and better every year, which means more time and more money invested in them.

I've been told I'm quite a performer. I've done musical theatre as a very high level of excellence and feel quite at home onstage in front of people. I enjoy doing a church Christmas or Easter production as much or more than anyone. But I've also been at churches that put hundreds of thousands of dollars into a show, when spiritually the church was dying. They ignored discipleship and outreach but wouldn't hear of missing a year performing their Singing Christmas Tree. It was maddening to witness people's idolatry of this sort of "golden calf".

For all our showbiz techniques and productions, what God really desires is authentic worship from His kids. When my oldest daughter was a preschooler, she would start marching around me in a circle when I came home, singing "I love my Daddy!" Honestly, the quality of her choreography and intonation of her song left much to be desired. Yet there is no other memory from her childhood that means more to me than that.

Why? Because she was singing out for all the world to hear about how much she loved me.

No matter how old you may be, you are God's child in whom He delights. Like any father, He loves to hear His children sing. Most of all, He loves it when they are singing about how much they love Him! What does He desire from their performance? He desires a sincere expression of what is in their hearts, He wants them to give Him their best, and for them not to be ashamed to express their love for Him in front of others. But a polished performance is of little interest to Him; in fact, any pretension about their gifts will take away from His enjoyment of their worship.

To be clear: excellence in worship is important and Biblical. We shouldn't ask for God to anoint something that is an inferior sacrifice. But if we focus on passionately worshipping God through our music, we then won't get so uptight about whether we played the piece perfectly.

I remember discussing this with one of my accompanists who would regularly torture himself if he played an occasional wrong note. I assured him, "I do want you to be prepared for every service. But more than that, I want you to be completely focused on worshipping God while you are playing. If you happen to miss a note or two, so what?"

Evidently, this little chat liberated him. He went on to play with much more ease, now that his focus had been taken off his performance and on to the One he was performing for.

Focusing on performance for me would be much easier than depending on the Lord. I know the kind of songs that gets the desired response, and I know what gets a response from the congregation. It would really feed my ego and love of attention as well.

But that's the difference in a "performance" and a "worship service". When we "perform", the goal is to get everyone's attention on us. But real worship is about focusing everyone's attention on God.

I saw one of the best examples of this principle when a choir visited my church once. We were having a Bible conference, and our pastor had invited a little choir from a neighboring state to come and sing.

When I saw the size of the choir and orchestra, I was not impressed. I was even less impressed when they started playing. Intonation, rhythm, missed notes...it was horrible. And when the choir joined in, they were just as bad. Few trained voices, lots of lazy rhythms and singing under the pitch. Not impressive at all.

But as the evening wore on, I noticed something. God had started working through the music on my spirit. I became surprised that, even though the quality level never changed, something was happening in the room and inside me. Suddenly, I found myself stunned as tears began flowing down my face! As the night progressed, I was weeping like a baby. It was embarrassing, and yet wonderful.

Why had the musical affected me so dramatically? Because these people, all mediocre musicians at best, were prayed up and asking God to show up. They had decided that God, not they, should get the glory. God then responded by doing something through them that a professional symphony and choir could not have accomplished.

More than any fad or gimmick, the presence of God will accomplish more than anything we can do in our own strength. When we depend on Him, He takes all our combined gifts and transforms them into a grand symphony, each one an instrument in His hands.

THE POWER OF A WORSHIPPING CHOIR

Although the movie "Sister Act" is admittedly not theologically deep, it has an ingredient that all churches would be most blessed to possess. Remember the scene where Whoopi Goldberg's character leads the choir for the first time in Sunday Mass. Instead of their usual bland style of music, the new director injected a huge dose of JOY! This Sunday for the first time, smiles permeated the platform, spilling over the cracked varnish of the pews, and ran out into the streets.

Guess what happened then? All the people outside in the street CAME INSIDE THE CHURCH, most of them probably for the first time! Why did they suddenly show up for church? Because there was finally enthusiasm in the building! And when there is LIFE and JOY and CELEBRATION, even the biggest sinner knows that he wants some of it.

How amazing that, even in a Hollywood movie, the world admits they'd be happy to show up at our churches if they only knew God was going to be in the room too. Even that Hollywood screenwriter knew that if God is in the house, the world will beat the doors down trying to get in.

How sad that they know what God's own children often forget.

Instead of joy, our churches go for the slick. Instead of praise, we strive to be professional. We have tried to look and act just like the world, replacing our worship with secular songs, replacing our offerings with "Don't feel obligated to give", and replacing the choir with a team of slim young people. We have mortgaged all the things that made us unique, so that we wouldn't seem strange to the folks that weren't there in the first place.

Now we are just like them, so much so we've convinced them we don't have anything they don't already possess!

Have you noticed what they do on TV awards shows when they want to really sell a song? What do they do to put their big inspirational numbers over the top? They bring out a choir, usually in traditional robes, singing strong and loud behind the soloist.

Yes, that's what I said… a choir. You remember those, don't you? Those antiquated artifacts of church life from way back when. Those musical dinosaurs most experts tell us are just taking up space on the platform that could be better used for a new video wall. And yet, when the world wants to celebrate and inspire joy, they do what is only natural – they call in the choir!

Back in 2020, people were making a lot of predictions about how the pandemic would affect the church. One thing most all the prognosticators guaranteed was that choirs were history. Seriously, how could you rationalize 50+ people spitting germs right at the congregation? Churches painted the walls to the choir loft black and demolished the risers. Entire choral music companies went out of business.

But guess what started picking back up within just about a year? Choir attendance.

Sure, it's not back to where it was. People have been predicting the death of the choir for the past 30 years or more. The "experts" have made any of us who resisted "the inevitable march of time" feel like fools for continuing to try. But it's now clear they only die if you do everything you can to kill them, which is exactly what many churches have done! So why are some churches so eager to pull the plug on them?

One reason is that we're just lazy. Choirs require a commitment from a large number of people. It takes work to keep people coming to rehearsal and worship week after week, year-round. But once you get used to having a strong choir in the service, any worship time without one seems like it has had the power drained out of it. And if a church is trying to soft-sell commitment, it can be a real chore to keep a choir going. It's easier for a "church-lite" congregation to just find a few good-looking, talented young people (some of which may be paid) to commit to leading weekly worship.

By the way, that's also less people you have to buy music for, and less of a music library to maintain. Also, if your worship leader doesn't have to prepare for and lead a choir, your church can get by with paying some dude with a guitar to lead on merely a part-time salary.

Not only laziness and expense, but another sad reason is the Church's love affair with worship fads. Choirs have gotten a stodgy image, and I admit that some of them deserve it. A lot of what's in your average church's choral library is "elevator music", with a homogenized, corny sound.

Suburban churches need to take a look at the African American churches whose choirs shake the walls every Sunday. Many worship leaders need to take the time to painstakingly transition their choir from singing dusty "anthems" to fresh soul-stirring ballads. But instead, they've stood by as the "old wineskins" broke apart. What could have been recast with a new mission and vision has been trashed.

That's too bad, because a choir can do things that a praise team just can't. For one thing, there are some songs that just don't sound the same with fewer people. Majestic hymns like "How Great Thou Art" and even some modern worship choruses don't have the same power with 6 people singing as they would with 60. As a result, we have greatly limited the music we can use when we give the choir their walking papers.

A choir is also a terrific training ground for new singers. There are lots of people who could one day be fine soloists or praise team members, but they have no "laboratory" in which to sharpen their gifts. Choirs offer a first step to the timid and untrained, so they can hone their skills in a supportive environment.

There are also some people who will never be great soloists, but nevertheless are called by God to lead worship with their exuberant spirit and their visual expressiveness. When the congregation sees all different kinds of people worshipping God, some of whom look just like them, they just can't help but join in the celebration.

My life was forever changed by a black choir. Years ago, I was a youth pastor in a Midwestern city. My desire for passionate worship had kept me working with youth, because the adult worship in the churches I had served was usually pretty cold.

One of my Sunday School teachers told me about a group of workers at a local plant who met each week during their lunch break to sing as a choir. But they needed a pianist who could play by ear and would come and play for free. When I showed up to do my friend a favor, I discovered I was the sole Anglo in the room.

As we started working on the music, I noticed their director didn't conduct by waving his arms in a time pattern like I was trained in school. He had all sorts of little signals and cues, and he would jab his fists at the choir to accentuate the rhythms in the piece.

These wonderful people who could have seen me as a poser trying to play "their music" accepted me whole-heartedly. What was most striking was the joyful abandon of their singing. They had twice the volume level of the "white" choir at the church I served, which was many times their size. And the expressions on their faces were beautiful.

I found a passion in the music that challenged me as much as it invigorated me. As I would drive back to my job at my predominantly white church one day, my eyes filled with tears. I wondered why worship couldn't be like that every Sunday.

It was then I knew God was calling me to focus completely on worship, and to strive for the passion that I had seen in my friends at the plant. And I learned a lesson that's stuck with me to this day. If all our churches showed that much love for God in their worship, the world would not be able to resist!

I am convinced that if we truly want people from all different backgrounds to feel welcomed, we must adapt the way we do worship. Our music must be accessible to all people, not just to white southerners from the Bible Belt. I think God wants us to do the type of worship that we will be doing in heaven - worship representing all cultures, led by worshippers of all races, lifting up the name of Jesus to every nation!

If you've been thinking about putting your choir out of its misery, I'd like to encourage you to reconsider. The best reason I can give you to do that is simply this: **choirs are Biblical**. A quick trip to II Chronicles 20 will illustrate that.

Most of us know at least the pertinent details of King Jehoshaphat and his predicament. His kingdom was about to be attacked by forces too strong for him to resist with his conventional army. When he recognized he was powerless to fight against such a huge army, he humbled himself before God and called on his people to pray for God's deliverance.

Instead of fighting, God told the king to simply "stand still" in faith and trust, and he would soon "see his salvation". While those words sound pretty spiritual to us right now, it might not seem like the most practical advice to a king facing destruction at the hands of a mighty enemy. But God reminds him that the battle is not his - "the battle is the Lord's" (vs. 15). Since the king had humbled himself and asked God's help, God took up their problem as His own and determined to make a way for His people.

What did God decide was the best way to answer their prayer that would also bring Him the most glory? His plan was to show them how puny their weapons were compared to His strength. The way He would do that is by sending the choir into battle first – in front of the army!

I wonder how many people showed up for choir practice after Jehoshaphat announced that new military strategy!

While this plan might seem ludicrous to any typical army general, it made sense on the battlefield of spiritual warfare. Instead of relying on their own military power, the choir leading the way with praise showed they relied on God's power alone to save them. I know some pastors and worship leaders who need to learn that lesson! Instead of relying on our talent, our budgets, our numbers, or our extravaganzas, we need to put our personal arsenals aside and take up our song of worship! Unless God shows up in the power of His presence, our churches are just buildings and our worship is a sad charade.

That battle formation is a perfect picture of how we enter into worship every Sunday. The choir is not a performance organization; it is a tool for spiritual warfare leading the charge against the Enemy. Satan hates Godly worship, so we are storming the gates of hell when we take up our song of praise to our Champion. It is not our programs that are going to defeat the forces of evil; it is our God rescuing us when we cry out to Him. Our worship says that we are depending on Him to win the victory, not on our own strength. And when we lay down our weapons and take up our song, God responds to His children… in a huge way!

> *"Now when they began to sing and to praise, the Lord set ambushes against the people…and they were defeated." - Vs. 22*

Notice that they didn't just sing: they began to "praise". Lots of churches sing songs about God each Sunday, but the ones where God shows up are the churches that are truly giving God praise. Many praise teams have perfectly coiffed hair, and many choirs sing with the most accurate diction. Yet God responds to churches that put their hearts and minds on Him above all things during worship.

Jehoshaphat's people were also willing to sing God's praise right in the face of their unbelieving enemies who surround them. They risked looking ridiculous, not to mention losing their lives, to show their dependence on the Lord. So God will also show up when, in the face of opposition inside or outside the church, we boldly lift Him up in the face of the opposing opinions of others.

In this Bible story, God wants us to learn to put down the suit of armor we've been protecting ourselves with and put on praise instead. He wants us to put down the weapons the world has convinced us are smart and up to date, and instead take up our song. When we start seeing our hearts as the true battlefield and worship as the true weapon, then we stop fighting each other and start fighting together.

God has given each of us a powerful song to sing: the testimony of the wonders He has done in our lives. And that testimony has the power to send demons sprawling across the floor disoriented and destroyed. When we take up our song, we encourage each other to keep in the fight.

On one side of the sanctuary, there may be someone facing a huge struggle. It might be their health, their job, or their family that's falling apart. But then they see a fellow believer that has gone through the fire, singing to the top of their lungs "The Goodness of God". A young adult struggling with depression and singleness sees a friend in the alto section with the very same challenges in life, singing their praise right in the midst of their doubts. Across the room, a senior citizen facing cancer treatment looks into the face of an older man in the choir loft who has just lost his wife, and yet he proclaims, "The Longer I Serve Him… the sweeter He grows"!

The choir is a singing, worshipping army for spiritual warfare, using our testimonies as the weapons to fight for the hearts of our congregation!

Our praise doesn't just send the Enemy into disarray. Worship has the power to take our focus off our problems and put it on the One who holds our lives in His hands. And when we look to Him, our perspective changes and we see things as they truly are.

So next time you feel the urge to take the battle into your own hands, take up your song instead. Next time you wish you could take the easy way out, take up your song. When you want to take up an offense with your brother, take up your song.

And when you are starting to take God's blessings for granted, take up your song and praise God just for who He is! That's when you'll see your world changed by the power of worship.

STANDING IN THE (GENERATION) GAP

The fact that there have been battles going on about worship style in our churches is well known. Unfortunately, it often comes down to different age groups having conflicting perceptions of what worship should be. While some modern worship leaves much to be desired in the theology department, very little of how we worshipped in the past was based on descriptions of worship in the Bible. In each case, personal preferences are put on a pedestal, replacing the supremacy of the Lord.

How odd it must be for God to have styles of music given more priority in our worship than He is.

Hymns vs. Worship Choruses

One of the most common ways the argument begins is in debating the merits of traditional hymns vs. new worship choruses. The differences in hymns and choruses are most specifically ones based on the following criteria:

1. Musical style - hymns are generally older than choruses. The hymns reflect an older style of music, and the choruses are similar to more modern forms of popular songwriting.
2. Poetic style - hymns generally have three to five verses (or stanzas) with a repeated chorus (or refrain) following each verse. Worship choruses have fewer verses (usually just two, if any) along with a repeated chorus, and perhaps a bridge leading back to the chorus again.

Theological comparisons

As far as a theological difference, worship choruses have a reputation as being less theological than hymns. The reality is that, with fewer if any verses, worship choruses by structure have less time to state lengthy theological ideas than the verses present in the average hymn. But don't let that make you fall for the argument that hymns are superior because of this depth of theology.

No worship songs (neither hymns nor worship choruses) were meant simply to be theological treatises set to music. To cast them as such is to lose their beauty and true purpose. Worship songs, both hymns and choruses, are meant to give praise and worship to God.

If tomorrow I wrote a song that presented every single Biblical doctrine, I doubt anyone would ever take the time to sing such a monstrosity. Just because a song is theologically sound doesn't mean it is successful at focusing the heart of the worshipper on God. And it most certainly doesn't make it a good song. Some of the best theology in our hymn books is found in songs that are unremembered to even the most senior of adults, and many of them are never sung at all. That's because some are simply not well written.

It is true that many worship choruses have been born from the Charismatic movement's emphasis on God's presence in worship. While we must be grateful for their revival of focus on worship, we do have to be careful to check for statements that reflect theology that conflicts with a responsible interpretation of scripture.

But this same standard must be applied to many of our established hymns, and several of them do not survive this test. Some of Charles Wesley's revered hymn lyrics have statements that imply we can lose our salvation, or that we can attain a state of sinless perfection in this present life (as in "Take away our bent to sinning" from "Love Divine, All Loves Excelling"). Even one verse of the beloved "Jesus Loves Me" states, "If I love Him when I die, He will take me home on high".

Worship choruses have spent a lot of time basking in the "presence of the Lord" and extolling the benefits of experiencing the Holy Spirit, but they have often lacked focus on the cross of Christ and other important theological topics.

However, the common criticism that most choruses are just "7/11 songs" ("seven words sung eleven times over") is not a valid criticism. Psalm 136 repeats the phrase "His mercy endures forever" a whopping 26 times. One thing that any teacher knows is repetition is a key to learning.

Likewise, while hymns may include more theology ideas, they have also tended to talk "about" God rather than talk "to Him". While the Psalms do speak of the attributes of the Lord, they also speak to him one on one, often in a personal and intimate manner that is missing in many hymns.

We need to understand this from a theological point of view: neither hymns nor choruses are "inspired directly by God". Only the holy scriptures (The Bible) are authoritatively inspired by God. If we neglect singing a hymn, we have not sinned. If we neglect scripture, then we invite sin. If we reject a chorus, we are not heretics. But if we reject a part of scripture, we have called a curse upon ourselves.

Stylistically and linguistically, some hymns belong to a completely different era. One of my favorite hymns is "Be Thou My Vision", but all the "thee-s" and "thou-s" eventually become quite a tongue-twister. As much as I love them, some hymns are just not great examples of basic songwriting. Here's an evaluation from C.S. Lewis in "Answers to Questions on Christianity" from his book *God In The Dock*:

> *"I dislike very much their hymns, which I consider to be fifth-rate poems set to sixth-rate music."*

Occasionally, a well-meaning Christian friend asks if I know the theology of some of the composers of worship choruses. I usually answer them with some harder question: *"So you know the theology and lifestyle of all the hymnwriters? How far do you plan to investigate a composer's personal life and commitment level?"*

If an absolute standard of purity were demanded before we could sing any composer's worship song or hymn, we would eventually end up not singing any songs. The truth is we simply cannot know the heart of any composer. But what I can know are the words to a particular hymn or chorus. If the words are theologically correct and the music is edifying to the congregation, I have no qualms about leading it in a worship service.

The undeniable truth is that while some hymns and choruses will live past us, some will inevitably die with this generation. But this is not a fact to be mourned, but a reality that we must embrace if we are to minister to this generation and the next. Despite all our protests, the music that survives will be whatever touches the hearts and souls of today's Christian and tomorrow's as well.

Ultimately, everything from this world is going to burn. What any mortal can create in this life won't hold a candle to the music of heaven. If you're expecting to hear "Amazing Grace" when you walk into heaven, you might better brace yourself. But don't worry.

One look into the face of Jesus and you won't care what music is playing!

THE PROBLEM OF INTIMACY

I have noticed a strange phenomenon when leading a hymn during worship. A lot of times, to make the hymn more accessible or just for the creative joy of it, I've placed the hymn in a more contemporary style while still keeping it singable for the average person. Occasionally I've been shocked when someone comes up and says, "That was nice, but could we please sing a hymn sometime in the service?"

They look just as shocked when I say, "We just did." What are we missing here?

Both of us are saying the same thing but meaning something completely different. When I say, "a hymn", I mean any older song not written in popular style, but in the four to five stanza style of the past. I love to read the words of some of the great hymns to soak up the meaning, and I enjoy finding a new way to arrange them musically.

Unfortunately, that is not what some church members mean by "a hymn". In their minds, there's a picture from childhood of the old home church. They see some fellow get up and say, "Let's stand and sing all four verses of hymn #475, "Victory in Jesus." As soon as he said that, the organ would crank up the last four to eight measures of that hymn, the choir would stand in unison with hymn books placed respectfully at their chests. Then the congregation would then sing all those stanzas exactly as they were written. If you forgot what number the hymn was, you could look up at the wooden board on the wall and see every hymn number for that day (as well as the Sunday School attendance and offering).

That actually didn't matter, because you knew from memory that #475 was "Victory In Jesus" in the hymnbook anyway. As the choir and congregation sang, the Music Minister would beat a time pattern in the air. We weren't sure why he did that – I wondered if it were the Baptist equivalent for the Catholic "sign of the cross" (it really looks about the same, especially in 4/4 time!).

So when I go straight out of a chorus directly into that hymn, with no fanfare or organ introduction, and do it with electric piano, bass and drums, it's not what they're expecting. Those sweet older adults are thinking, "Well, this chorus does seem a little more familiar, but when are we going to do a hymn?!"

When that happens, and it does, it tells me something important. They don't want me just to do a hymn. They want me to make it 1955 again. Sorry, I'm not even going to try and do that.

I understand they miss the "trappings" of their childhood church, and they wish that worship could be a connection to their memories of the past. For many, the best worship would be a weekly "trip down memory lane", wallowing in nostalgia that soothes the soul but never edifies the spirit.

The believer who focuses only on the past will likely be oblivious to what God is doing today. Therefore, winning new people to

Christ and keeping the work of the church going will be of lesser importance. If the church ignores the needs of this present generation, then our pews will be populated by only those of the past generation.

That is a recipe for extinction.

The Problem with Contemporary Worship

Rick Warren, when asked why there was no organ in his church, famously made the observation, "How many people listen to organ music in their cars?" The answer is most likely "only organists". Warren's assumption is that if we want people to be able to worship easily, we need to use music they enjoy. The common sense of this argument is undeniable.

However, in their attempt to make worship music that your average church member can enjoy, much of it sounds like second-rate U2 from the 1990s. Far from being the "devil rock music" we were warned about, it is now punishingly generic. Songs are so similar that worship sites like Multitracks.com offer a droning "synth pad" that can be added to the start of most every worship song in any key. One size fits all.

As a musician who often leads worship from the piano, I find myself adding more interesting passing chords to the 3 or 4 chords most songs allow. I simply get bored playing many of them, especially when there is little rhythmic variation (no soul, no funk, etc.). Every one of them is so very "white". Worship can feel like going to the same restaurant every day and eating the same meal, over and over again.

Growing up in a Bible Belt church, I was always taught everyone should glorify God with their gifts in the church! However, that extended only those who sang or played a particular style of music. There was no room for jazz or Latin influence, and we homogenized anything that came out of Black Urban churches, smoothing out all the rhythms. Poor Andrae Crouch – his brilliant funky songs were massacred by our white pianists!

And music was the only one of the Arts allowed: absolutely no room for dance or drama! Like Calvin, who reacted against the voluptuous renaissance art by painting sanctuaries a dull white, we seemed to want our worship plain and dry to not make the Lord look boring by comparison. As if that were possible.

Modern worship needs to not only focus on correct Biblical theology in our music. We need to encourage and nurture Christian artists who too often get little support in the local church. Like a good chef would prepare tasty food, we need to welcome a little spice in our worship diet. Why would anyone want only white bread and vanilla pudding?

The Problem with Hymns

I've noticed that not only do some more traditional members prefer hymns, but they have an unusually strong dislike for choruses. I wondered why this was, because I would get the same reaction from these people even when I used "easy listening" style choruses. The focus of their disdain was not as much a dislike of musical style as often a disdain for the intimacy of the chorus's words in their expression of love to the Father.

You see, hymns (with a few exceptions like "In The Garden") generally keep God at a safe distance. They tend to talk about God, not to Him. Many in the WWII generation brought with them to church a strong sense of duty. For them, God is the general and attending church is their duty.

While there is an amount of honor in that, it is not what the Father truly desires. His heart is that we come to Him out of love. But for that generation, the choruses seem too "syrupy" and speak to God with too much familiarity. To them, that familiarity implies a lack of respect and dignity. With the hymns, they are allowed to stay a good arms-length distance from God.

This is also reflective of our changing view of fatherhood. Today, fathers are expected to be nurturing, loving, and affectionate with their children. But many fathers in the past, while deeply loving their children, came off as more distant and aloof. They didn't help with the kids much, leaving most of the child-rearing to the mothers.

This view of a distant, unknowable father affects your image of your Heavenly Father. When we enter into intimate expressions of love toward the Father in worship, it all seems somehow inappropriate and wrong to them. The formality of traditional worship keeps us from getting sloppy all over God. We cannot imagine He would actually want to be around us, and desire to experience His children, warts and all. Out of respect we cover ourselves in the trappings of formality, thinking we give God a break from the mess of our lives.

While the issue of intimacy is a major stumbling block for many traditional worshippers, it is one that can be overcome. When pastors endeavor to preach on worship, real changes can occur in all generations.

I will never forget one Sunday, watching a senior adult gentleman in my choir as he worshipped. The way he was raised said that you never clapped in church, never showed emotion, never stepped "out of the box". Yet here he was, clapping along with all his might to the uptempo worship chorus we were singing that weekend. You could tell that he was a little unsure of the beat, but he didn't care. He just wanted to be a part of what God was doing that Sunday in worship, and he didn't mind if that meant going beyond his personal comfort zone!

Have it your way

The greatest tragedy within the "worship wars" is the imbalance that the debate has brought on in the Body of Christ. With each side clamoring to get their own way, church leaders are scrambling to reach a suitable compromise. The most popular solution has been to start a "contemporary service" and a "traditional service", with the hopes that we can separate the combatants like you would children fighting on the playground (and that's a good picture of the lack of maturity present in this fight). This way everybody gets what they want.

Everyone except the Lord.

Jesus said His desire was that His followers would be one, just as He and the Father are one. But if we start separating people by musical taste within our church fellowship, we miss out on what the other members bring to the Body of Christ: their gifts, their perspective, and their collective spiritual experience.

How much of a stretch would it be if we all figured out that worship isn't just for us? As we are starting to rediscover, worship is for God …we just get the honor of joining in the chorus that heaven and earth is singing! How hard would it be for all those mature older adults to realize that the living God will not allow worship to stay in 1955? How difficult would it be for younger adults to value where God has brought us from by worshipping through the majesty of hymns?

When will we all realize that to God, none of it is very important. But what He most certainly doesn't want is the way we are "worshipping our style of worship".

CREATIVE DIFFERENCES

You remember the dumbest things from childhood. Mine was a PE coach. Not that she was dumb, but that she did something completely innocuous that emotionally destroyed me one day.

I was maybe in third or fourth grade, standing in a line to come in from the playground. I suppose the PE teacher had said be quiet, but I was turned talking to another child. It was then she came over and gave me what was at the most a little pat of correction on the bottom.

Though I felt no pain, the fact she'd shown disapproval utterly crushed me. I remember going home and blubbering to my mom as if I'd been beaten with a tire iron. I think she even called the principal. I only hope that poor teacher didn't get in trouble for hurting my puny little feelings.

Now, it would be easy to blame my extreme overreaction on my relationship with my dad, who was emotionally distant and a harsh disciplinarian. But the truth was it had nothing to do with that. It was completely to do with me…

I'm sensitive. There, I said it.

If my wife is reading this right now, she's rolling her eyes because she knows it better than anyone. Lord, please give her patience.

Any criticism I get as a minister (and that's a regular part of the gig) will honestly devastate me for a while. Every time someone leaves the church, sleep is lost. The offhand remarks most people brush off after a moment's time, I twist and turn over for days.

It's a curse. And a blessing.

This is what is known as an "artistic temperament". That's how creative people get labeled when they are seen as overreacting. Just talk to any boss and you'll find the staff members they have the most conflict with tend to also be the most creative ones.

> *"All I told the worship pastor was that the new song he did Sunday wasn't my favorite. Now he won't make eye contact with me!"*

If that sounds familiar, you probably crushed his soul though you didn't mean to. He loves that new song and thought it would set your sermon up perfectly. Heck, he may have even written it and didn't tell you.

No, it's not your fault. It's just the flip side of his gift.

When you are a "creative", the upside of your *sensitivity* is part of what makes you great at artistic expression. When you sing a song you love, your sensitivity means the passion will spill over the top and into the congregation. They'll be moved and God will infuse the song with His Spirit to heal many.

Your art works so well specifically because you're so sensitive. Because you feel things more deeply and intensely than others, that intensity gives your art power.

But…that same sensitivity can make you overreact in the extreme sometimes. Even when others communicated correction in the kindest possible way, it can crush you. It makes no sense to those around you. They tried to be gentle. And yet, you're still destroyed and feel rejected.

It's funny how God uses that sensitivity, even when wounded, to create something beautiful. I remember one Christmas something happened during the day that crushed me emotionally, but I had to go play for a group of carolers the same night. I sat down at the piano to play some very non-challenging carols, very basic arrangements. But because my emotions were raw, I played with a level of passion the event didn't really call for. I brooded over the keys, pouring my soul into something I wouldn't have been thinking much about normally.

I remember the carolers all applauding, but with rather dazed looks on their faces!

I hate to admit it but I was pretty awesome that night. And ironically, that's because I was hurting. I've also noticed I preach some of my best sermons after people have ticked me off before the service. Give me a little opposition, get me a little riled up and whoa Nelly! It's gonna be a fun Sunday!

But there's a big downside to the artistic temperament. This is why so many actors and musicians struggle with *depression, substance abuse, and often suicide*. When you're wired so extremely, you do great art. But without spiritual healing and discipline that comes from God, you can become self-destructive and burn out early.

King David is the perfect Biblical example of this kind of personality. He was a warrior on one hand but wrote tremendous poetry and songs in his solitude. There was a common denominator in both his fighting and his songwriting.

What was that common denominator? **Passion**.

If you look, you can see his mood swings all through the Psalms. He'll go from a joyous explosion of worship in one to wallowing in self-doubt in another. And look out for what theologians call the "imprecatory Psalms". Those are the ones where he's so mad at his enemies, he's asking God to do crazy stuff like smash their kid's heads on the rocks!

When he nearly destroyed his kingdom through sexual sin with Bathsheba, he evidences the need of creatives for discipline in their lives. It was only after he got out of a routine and neglected his kingly responsibilities that he was tempted into an affair. Then add to that his murderous attempt at coving it up. His lack of control caused one man to lose his life.

But even with all his extremes and horrible sins, the Bible calls him "a man after God's heart". How can so much potential for both good and bad be in one person? Well, it has to do with whether that person has learned to let the Spirit of God lead and discipline them.

If the person I've been describing sounds like you, you're in great need of something you probably avoid at any costs: spiritual discipline.

Most creatives I know are naturally wired as free spirits. We dislike rules or anything that puts boundaries around us. What we don't often realize is boundaries are in fact our friends. It's when the governors are completely taken off and boundaries are crossed that we get into trouble and careen out of control.

Interestingly, we also create better art within boundaries. If you ask me to write a song, I'll ask you what about. If you say, "Oh, anything", that's the worst answer you could give. Because without a clear goal and specific borders, I'll flail about and probably not end up writing anything. But if you say, "Write a love song about autumn", you'll have something in less than a day! That's because I know specifically where to head – you have given me a defined boundary that keeps me from wasting time.

Specific parameters help focus the artist on his goal. And defined boundaries in the creative's personal and spiritual life work in the same way. They keep us on-task and from giving in to excess and self-indulgence.

The way to deal with your own artistic temperament is to first acknowledge you have one. Understand that your reaction will often tend toward the extreme. Know that how you want to react is probably about 25% more than what the situation truly calls for.

Also, find someone you trust and become accountable to them for your spiritual health. If they are a friend, they probably already know some of your tendencies but just don't have a name for them yet. Give them permission to talk with you honestly when they see you operating in the extreme.

Most of all, STAY IN THE WORD OF GOD. Seriously, this is not just "preacher talk". God will speak to you through His Word and talk you off the ledge if you'll listen. But if you let depression or excess cause you to ignore God, you make it harder for Him to speak to you. So a daily discipline of prayer and Bible Study may save your spiritual life.

It might just save your physical life as well. It shouldn't come as a surprise that artistic people are prone to depression and substance abuse. Note, I'm not saying all creatives have drug problems – I'm only saying many struggle with substances that strongly affect the emotions. When you feel pain deeply, you may try to self-medicate that pain. Understand that Satan will use this very thing to try and destroy you, especially if you work in a ministry.

For Satan, the fact you are so creative makes the stakes high. Your creativity reflects the nature of your Creator, so your Enemy will hate that about you. He'll try and use your sensitivity, the very thing through which God has gifted you, to destroy you.

Just remember when you're hurting, that's just the downside of your gift. Pain is the price you pay for having God work through you in such a dynamic way. God can use you greatly because of it, but not if you forfeit your calling because you lack discipline.

Understand yourself and do what David did. When everyone had turned against him, the Bible says David "encouraged himself in the Lord" (1 Sam 30:6). Seems he had learned from experience how to ignore what he was feeling and trust what God was saying instead.

Your feelings are a true gift, but your faith is the greatest gift. When you have to choose between the two, go with faith every time. It may just save your gift, and your life.

STRANGE FIRE

God will not grant us His presence if He knows we will misuse it. Such was the problem with Nadab and Abihu, two of Aaron's sons, who decided from the way the people responded to their dad that this worship-leading gig was a pretty cool thing. So they decided to give it a try themselves…

> *"And Nadab and Abihu, the sons of Aaron, took either of them his censer, and put fire therein, and put incense thereon, and offered strange fire before the LORD, which he commanded them not." Lev 10:1*

God showed them that worship is nothing to be trifled with, and He sent fire to vaporize both of Aaron's sons! You'd think we would have learned from this not to play around with the holy things of God as if they were common.

But Aaron's boys were not the only ministers who tried to use God's power for their own purposes. Simon the Sorcerer (Acts 8:9-24), who used Satan's techniques to make things happen, saw the power Jesus' followers displayed and decided he wanted in on the action. He attempted to buy a "partnership" in this new spiritual franchise. But he was quickly informed that the power of God was not for sale!

Yet our church leaders will use every trick in the book - church growth strategies, money, preaching and musical gifts - to make a sad imitation of what only God can accomplish through his power and anointing.

Just listen to the pastor down the block who preaches the sermons of his hero at the TV megachurch, thinking the same words will bring similar results. Watch the worship leader who mixes songs in a service like ingredients in a cauldron, thinking that just the right combination will invite the Spirit just like on his favorite worship CD.

Their techniques may not be much different than the incantations Simon the Sorcerer used to manipulate the lives of gullible people. They want a semblance of God's power so they can claim it as their own, but God refuses to be owned.

I watched a worship service of a church I know well on the internet recently. It had been known for powerful worship in the past, and a big joyful choir. Clearly God had worked in this church in a dynamic way for many years.

But since moves of God are hard to sustain, over the years the choir and the church had dwindled. They began spacing choir members further and further apart to cover up the declining enrollment. Leadership had changed hands several times over. With all the changes, they struggled to hold onto the spirit of praise that had once permeated the sanctuary.

Sound anything like your church?

This particular Sunday, they'd invited former choir members to return and sing with them for a special occasion. They performed some of the old numbers God had used in the church's past. As the orchestra struck up the notes to an old favorite, I sat back in my chair ready for God's presence to take charge once again…

Except, it didn't.

As I watched, I couldn't decide what exactly was wrong. All the former ingredients were in place. The singers were rehearsed and ready, the instruments in tune and on the beat. Soloists sang well and the director was competent in his leadership. I seriously doubt any participants were in spiritual rebellion against God. Their pastor wouldn't have allowed them to participate.

But the Spirit that had been there and taken over the proceedings before was glaringly absent, or at least greatly minimized. I think most everyone knew it, though few would be rude enough to say it out loud.

The presence and power of God in a church is a mercurial, unpredictable thing. For those of us who've led worship, understanding why dynamic worship happens or doesn't is often like trying to nail Jello to the wall. You can insert the same ingredients that before brought great life-change and commitment, but today all you may see is a faded copy of the glory that had been there in the past.

What makes the difference? What is the key? What is it that hinders God's movement in one service, and yet invites and welcomes it in another?

I asked that in my own church several years ago. I was not only the pastor but occasionally lead worship as well. The song I'd prepared for one Sunday had always been greatly used to draw people into worship in the past. I'd been saving it for my new congregation for almost a year now, expecting it would draw our people toward a deeper level of worship.

When the moment for the song came, I sang it passionately with a clear conscience before the Lord. As far as I could tell, both the Spirit and the delivery were God-honoring. But after the song was over, I could tell it had clearly made no impact at all. I might as well have been singing in a foreign language.

As the old expression goes, it went over like a lead balloon.

Worship is a great indicator of a church's love for God. Nothing betrays a church's health like a fever for God in worship. But that fever is something that must be caught, not just taught. All the doctrine can be right, all the notes sung and played perfectly, and yet…their heart are unmoved.

Nothing will happen of worth unless God's Spirit fills it all up.

Passionless worship is like a helium balloon that someone unknotted. It hisses and flails, eventually going limp: a shriveled, empty sack. Nothing is wrong with the balloon, except there's simply none of that "special air" lifting the balloon to the heavens.

Sure, we can try and blow it up with our own human air, which is what many churches do every Sunday. We can employ all the latest strategies, and use only the newest, most popular songs. But the balloon will never rise. Toss it in the air and it will fall straight to the ground. Human effort is of no use unless that special helium of God's Spirit is injected.

King David found this out the hard way in 2 Samuel 6 when he tried to move the Ark of the Covenant, the symbol of God's power and presence, back to Jerusalem after being captured by the Philistines. He thought he could just move it the most logical and convenient way, on an ox cart (the same way the pagans had done it). But he had ignored Moses' law that gave strict instruction that the Levite priests must move it on foot.

His honorable goal of returning God-centered worship to Jerusalem ended in the death of one of the transporters, who reached out to steady the Ark during a rough patch of ground. David learned the hard way that worship is not just a matter of our strategies, or how we prefer to do it.

Real worship is all about our obedience and submission to God. Moving that ark should not have been about the most convenient, preferred way to do it. It is not about "how we'd prefer to do it" or "what styles we're comfortable with". Those are irrelevant.

When all the ingredients seem to be there but passionate worship doesn't happen, we need to stop and ask ourselves some hard questions…

- why is God choosing not to enter into our worship?
- why is passion missing?
- what is standing in the way of God being in our midst and taking control, since He desires nothing more?

Could it be our balloon is limp with the air of human effort alone, and with no "heavenly breath"?

When worship doesn't happen, the problem is most often not in the performance of it, nor with the ingredients. The problem is uniquely spiritual. That's because worship was never meant to be about the feelings our music brings to people, nor about our professional strategies. It must start with a passion in our own hearts, a passion for God that is only using the music as a means to express itself.

But when we are spiritually impotent, all the notes can be there and yet our songs will still ring hollow. That's because the songs never held the power in the first place – they were only the carriers of the fever with which we've been stricken.

That fever is a longing for God Himself. But without that heat, nothing rises up to the throne room.

The problem with much of our worship is that we're just singing for our enjoyment and filling it up with our own desires. Whose air it's filled with makes all the difference as to whether our worship rises or falls.

And without a God-breathed passion within it, our worship is just a lot of hot air.

LOWERING YOUR SHIELDS

One of the things I've learned as a married man is while a woman may buy costume jewelry for herself, it is not a good idea for her husband to buy her anything that is not 100% authentic. If I gave my wife fake jewelry, it might send the message that my love for her is also less than authentic.

Likewise, the gifts we offer the Lord must be authentic. In John 4:24, Jesus Himself says that "God is Spirit, and those who worship Him must worship in spirit and truth." The "truth" part of that statement refers not only to worship being done according to the guidelines of Scripture, but also that we must be sincere in our worship and in our motive for worshipping.

King Rehoboam (2 Chronicles 12) was the son of Solomon, but greatly lacked the wisdom his father possessed. He ignored the advice of older wise counselors and listened to his buddies instead. This caused Israel to split away from the tribe of Judah. Because of his rejection of God's leadership, God allowed Shishak the King of Egypt to overrun Judah and the city of Jerusalem.

Later, thanks to Rehoboam's 11th hour repentance, God spared them from total annihilation. However, God did allow Shishak to ransack the King's house and the Temple, taking with him all the valuables of the Lord's house. Some of the most noticeable items missing after the siege were the 300 gold shields that were held by the Temple guards when the king went to worship. It is said these shields each contained around three pounds of solid gold and were so huge they would actually cover up the guards who were holding them.

In addition to their obvious beauty, their importance is emphasized by the fact that God himself had commanded them to be made for the Temple. Their absence was certainly a source of chagrin and a sad testimony to all of the spiritual condition of Judah.

However, Rehoboam found a solution. While they were in no financial condition to make new gold shields, he had his craftsmen create exact replicas of the original shields. Only this time, the shields were made of bronze. These was much cheaper but still had a shiny appearance.

But bronze needs constant polishing to keep its shine from tarnishing over time. The beauty that used to come naturally with the gold shields now was something that had to be propped up by long hours of labor. No matter how beautiful those bronze shields were, to the King's staff they were sad imitations of something that had before possessed a natural and easy beauty.

It is fitting that a story that has so much to do with the Temple ends up teaching us so very much about worship. In fact, Rehoboam's life is summed up in verse 14 of that same chapter by an indictment about his lack of authentic worship:

*"And he did evil, because **he did not prepare his heart to seek the Lord.**"*

His lack of personal obedience to God led directly to God's Temple being debased and devalued. By replacing the gold shields with bronze, he showed that his true concern was not the authenticity of his worship but only the appearance of his worship before men. When the focus of worship is moved from the Lord to the opinions of men, we have then ceased to worship God in either "spirit" or "truth".

So how does this relate to our worship in the Church today? Well, we have more than enough "bronze shields" of our own making.

THE SHIELD OF "PRODUCTION VALUES"

No one loves great technology more than me. I think God's church should be well equipped with the best and brightest lighting and sound available. While many churches are not able to meet the financial cost great technology brings, excellence should always be our goal.

However, I'm afraid some of us have begun to trust in these technical bells and whistles and their ability to manipulate people's emotions more than be rely on the Spirit of God to move in our midst. We've got everything so preplanned that there's no expectation or allowance for God to diverge from that plan. We are in control.

Also, many worship leaders preplan not only each song but each word said into a microphone. They want a slick presentation with no glitches. But when everything is prescribed, there's little room for the Holy Spirit to do something that not listed on the Planning Center order of service.

Planning ahead is important, of course. You don't want the train to run off the track. But if everything that happens in the service is only what human effort itself can achieve, that's a sad substitute for God's leadership. Our worship becomes little more than a vain work of our flesh.

THE SHIELD OF "PERFORMANCE"

I heard once about a music minister who told his choir and singers that they needed to "practice worshipping in front of a mirror". The reason was he said some of them didn't really "look like they were worshipping". Strangely enough, I know this choir to be one of the most expressive groups of worshippers I have ever seen. Still, he encouraged them to attempt to be more deliberately demonstrative in their expressions of worship, lifting their hands more and trying to "look joyful".

I've also been in churches where, in contrast to my reserved Baptist upbringing, the people were trained to act like they "feel the Spirit". It's like the old fable of the Emperor's New Clothes. Everyone tries to pretend they feel God's Spirit moving, or else others will think there's something wrong with them. So they weep, shout, and flail about when nothing spiritual is really going on. They do it because they don't want to get left out.

Worship, by its very nature, must come naturally as an authentic expression of the believer's heart. Anything forced negates the ability of the believer to truly worship. And the converse is true also, in that any Biblical expression of praise that is suppressed will drain worship of its sincerity. We must not worship based on the whims of men, whether that means those men would like to see a more emotional show, or that they would prefer something more restrained.

As Proverbs 29:25 clearly points out, *"The fear of man brings a snare, but whoever trusts in the Lord shall be safe".* That is especially true in worship.

When our eyes stray from the Lord onto others we will inevitably get tripped up, whether we "play up" to or "play down" to their desires. While I have seen a few worshippers whose personal "ticks" and expressions were somewhat distracting, self-consciousness in worship is rarely helpful either. I have also found that I get less distracted by others when I move from being a *spectator of worship* to a *participator in worship*.

God must be our focus, and our action of worship must be spontaneous, unrehearsed, and sincere.

THE SHIELD OF PERSONAL PREFERENCE

I used to tell people that worship is like a smorgasbord; there's something in each service for everybody. If you like hymns, don't worry...there'll be one for you any minute. If choruses are more to your taste, then we'll whip one up for you right after that hymn.

This explanation seemed levelheaded and inclusive of everyone, with one striking exception: God. While my little analogy usually made the people I was talking to happy, I doubt that it got many cheers in heaven.

I missed one of the basic tenets of worship: ***true worship is not about what I like, but it is most certainly about what God likes!*** And God has taken a lot of time in the Bible to let us know very clearly what He wants.

What God wants in worship is not about the style of music, because the Scriptures don't talk about style. While I've heard Christian speakers warn against using "worldly" styles of music, there really isn't a truly Christian style of music. Even the old hymn tunes were written in the musical styles that were popular in their era. Legend even says that Martin Luther used a barroom melody as the tune for "A Mighty Fortress Is Our God".

What the Bible does speak of is worship that is expressed through singing, the playing of instruments (with a lot of reference to percussive instruments, by the way), clapping, lifted hands, kneeling, bowing, laying prostrate, shouting, and...brace yourself... dancing. And what seems glaringly absent from this list are some expressions most church members are used to seeing in worship: folded arms, scowled faces, silent voices, downward glances.

Those folks might protest my criticism by saying, "That's just how I worship. I'm not comfortable with any expressiveness in public." But the right question here is not "what are you comfortable with", but "what is God comfortable with"?

We are not called to do what's "comfortable" for us, we are called to give outward expression to God in worship from a loving heart. True, different people express love in different ways, some being naturally more emotional than others. But if you tell me that you love your wife even though you don't kiss her or tell her you love her, I will probably laugh right in your face. If you tell me that you've never snuggled with your kids because the tradition you grew up in frowned on physical contact with your children, I'd recommend you see a counselor.

If you say that you don't make at least some expression to God in worship but you have a life-changing relationship with Him, I'm going to think that there's something not quite right with that relationship. It doesn't mean you're not a believer, just like not kissing your wife doesn't prove you don't love her. But it does indicate that something is wrong between the two of you, whether it's you and your wife…or you and your God.

PASSION FOR HIS PRESENCE

The Bible is filled with examples of how God responds not to our calculated reserve, but to our passion for Him. Who is it that Jesus says would be filled…The one who "hungers & thirsts after righteousness" (Matt 5:6).

Out of the whole crowd of people, Jesus noticed a little man named Zacchaeus who was bold enough to climb a tree in hopes of catching a glimpse of the Lord. Moses was not satisfied with talking audibly with God. He asked God, "Show me your glory", even though that would have meant certain death for his physical body.

And why does the Bible refer to David as "a man after God's own heart"? It certainly wasn't because of his record as a faithful husband and father! It was because of his heart for worship; a heart so passionate that he would sit directly before the presence of the Lord in the Tabernacle and worship, risking the disapproval of God. It was that intimacy of "Tabernacle of David" that God said He wanted to restore (Acts 15:16), not the formality and majesty of Solomon's Temple.

So, have you discovered your own shield? Whichever one it is, lay aside your polish and put those bronze shields back in the closet. If we lay down the imitation shields we've crafted, God will be faithful to replace them with gold that is purified in the sincerity and passion of true worship.

HOW MUCH "FREEDOM OF WORSHIP" IS TOO MUCH?

The flag ladies you'll find in some churches fascinate me. They're the equivalent of a church dance team, although there's no pelvic gyrating. Their feet hardly ever leave the floor... which keeps them from doing anything that might look like actual dancing.

I grew up Baptist, so dancing was always a big no-no, right up there with smoking, drinking, and dating a Methodist. It turns out some other denominations are just as uncomfortable with cutting a rug. Instead of dancing and "grieving the Spirit", they have flag teams that simply flap their arms in time with the music while holding brightly colored flags.

Warning: do not try this near an airport. Trust me on this one.

Also, they usually wear white or shiny silver dresses, often embroidered with gold trim and draped with a sparkly gold sash. You know, just like real angels wear! These "more modest cousins" of the leotard look like large white Snuggies and are designed specifically not to call attention to the female form.

Considering the age of most of those participating, this is merciful.

There are a few "flag guys" as well. These are usually husbands of the flag ladies who have done something so wrong, they're paying their way "out of the dog house" by participating. You can spot them easily – they're always that one awkward guy standing in the middle of 6 ladies. The rest of us men feel embarrassed for them and avert our eyes to look away from their shame.

The flags are attached to long poles (AUTHOR'S NOTE: do not under any circumstance refer to this as "pole dancing"). The performers twirl the poles in time with the music. Since the movements are easy and the music often prerecorded, this avoids the need for anyone with actual talent to participate.

Those poles can really leave a mark if you're not careful with them. Just take my word on this.

We once had a flag lady "go rogue" on us in one church. She left the safe confines of the cleared platform area (which was barren except for a few unfortunate ferns) and ventured down to the front floor area. Caught up in the throes of worship, she careened out of control once across the length of the front row, swinging her pole just over the heads of innocent congregants.

If this happens in your church, take the lady ("Rogue One" as we later referred to her) very seriously. Flag poles are really nothing more than large metal spears. They are capable of shish-kabobbing church members like a rhinestone-bedazzled Vlad the Impaler.

I believe flag ladies are good illustrations of why God allows churches to have different styles of worship. I know people criticize the number of different denominations, but I don't think it's necessarily a bad thing. Why? Because I have the option not to attend a church where worship is quite so life-threatening.

Now that we've all had a good laugh at their expense, here's an honest question. Do you think God enjoys their worship more or less than yours?

Before you answer too quickly, here's my problem. I'm a grown man who really should be past the age where I care what anyone thinks of me. I preach about taking a stand for your faith and not being ashamed of the Gospel of Jesus Christ. And yet…

This 6-foot, 2 inch tall, 200 and none-of-your-business pounds man would probably be too embarrassed to ever worship God as freely as those church ladies did. Sorry, but that's just the honest truth.

Of course I'd say the real reason is I don't believe God really wants me to pick up a gold flag and start flapping it. But what if He did? And how much of what I do in worship is more about what I'm "comfortable" with and not about what God wants?

It's easy to talk big about how much we love God and what our faith means to us. But recently a huge chunk of people who were going to church before Covid just disappeared. Was it the Rapture? I'm afraid not. It was just a whole bunch of professing believers who decided God wasn't worth the trouble of getting out of bed on a Sunday.

For all our big talk, all it took to kill our commitment to our churches was an extended "snow day".

In our cynicism and faux sophistication, it's easy to belittle the church ladies with their flags. The sad truth may be we just aren't passionate enough to make fools of ourselves if God wanted us to.

As Keith Green put it, "Jesus rose from the dead. And you can't even get out of bed!"

I'm feeling a little convicted right now by those flag ladies. I wonder if I'm really giving God the worship He desires, or am I doing just enough not to look silly?

Maybe those flag ladies had the right idea after all. Because if all you've got is a flag, you'd better waive it high. So what if the world thinks you look silly?

You were never supposed to be doing it for them anyway.

RAIDERS OF THE LOST ARK

If you want to find out who your real friends are, ask for help moving! Suddenly everyone has "plans" that day.

However, we have had a few folks show up when moving to new church. It's the perfect opportunity for nosy church members to rifle through the new pastor's sock drawer and estimate the cost of his wife's wardrobe.

Seriously, moving is one of the most stressful things you can do. We naturally look for the easiest way to get the job done. But if you've ever moved much, you know that doing things the easy way is not always best.

We moved once across country to East Tennessee but had to do the packing ourselves. I was young and didn't know to pad the furniture. When we arrived at our new home, I wondered why there seemed to be so much "sawdust" on the floor of the moving truck. Then my wife let me have it: the "sawdust" was the finish off of her dining room chairs. They had rubbed against each other for the entire trip!

King David found out the hard way just how tough moving is, especially when it involved something strategic to Old Testament worship: the Ark of the Covenant.

Everyone knows what the Ark is, thanks to that great Spielberg/Lucas film with Harrison Ford. While the Bible doesn't mention it sending out death rays and melting Nazi's faces off, it does say it was central to worship. The presence of God rested upon the Ark, hidden by the thick curtain in the Most Holy of Holies. It was a constant reminder that God was with Israel.

But the corrupt priests Hophne and Phinias took this sacred element of worship into battle with them, thinking having God on their side would tip the scales in their favor. But God is no fool, and they were both killed in battle. The Philistines proudly took the Ark into their possession, thinking they had captured Israel's God.

Boy, were they in for a surprise.

God struck the Philistines with tumors and cursed them with a rat infestation. When they looked into the Ark, over 50,000 men were struck dead. Then on top of all that, hemorrhoids (maybe I should have said "on bottom of all that"). They soon had had enough of Israel and this odd golden box, so they dumped the Ark and ran!

After 20 years of the Ark in exile, David's passion for worship inspires him to go and retrieve the Ark and return it to Jerusalem. But in spite of having the right motive, they went about getting the Ark the wrong way...

So they set the ark of God on a new cart, and brought it out of the house of Abinadab, which *was* on the hill; and Uzzah and Ahio, the sons of Abinadab, drove the new cart...Then David and all the house of Israel played *music* before the Lord on all kinds of *instruments of* fir wood, on harps, on stringed instruments, on tambourines, on sistrums, and on cymbals.

And when they came to Nachon's threshing floor, Uzzah put out *his hand* to the ark of God and took hold of it, for the oxen stumbled. Then the anger of the Lord was aroused against Uzzah, and God struck him there for his error; and he died there by the ark of God. - 2 Samuel 6:3-6

For all his passion for God, David moved the Ark the same way the Philistines had: on an ox cart. It was practical, it was easy, but it was not the way God had specifically prescribed for it to be moved. The vessel symbolizing the presence of God Himself was not supposed to be moved like your mom's favorite sofa!

The ox cart was a direct violation of the Old Testament requirement that the Ark be carried by staves and placed upon the shoulders of the men of Levi, of the family of Kohath (Num. 3:30-31; 4:15; 7:9; Exod. 25:14-15). Specifically, men set apart as priests for worship were to physically carry the Ark, by the sweat of their brows, to its new place of rest. Since it was a sacred object, it was never to be defiled by human hands.

Though Uzzah's action of reaching out to steady the Ark was understandable, he should have never had to steady it. If they had done it the way God said to do it, he would have never lost his life. So his death was not Uzzah's fault for touching the Ark, it was David's fault for not listening to the Word of God.

Do you see now where I'm going with this?

Many of you have grown up in denominations as I have known for their love of the Word of God. Yet how ironic when we say we love God, we revere His Word, but we neglect to worship Him the way he has prescribed!

David's sin was the same as ours today: presuming that God's worship should have anything to do with his convenience or preference. How we have bent over backwards to make people happy with multiple worship style options!

Don't like those new choruses? We've got a "classic worship" option where you can pretend it's 1955 all over again!

Don't like the hymns? Come to our contemporary service where the median age of attenders is younger than the smoke machine we use!

Don't feel like getting up? Just tune in on the live-stream and worship the Living God in your pajamas on the couch!

I'll never forget traveling to a church that wanted to hire me as their new worship leader. The pastor told me, "We've got a Saturday night Country service that you don't have to lead. Just watch it, and then you'll lead the Sunday morning service and we'll vote to call you to our church!"

When he said, "Country service", I assumed some old hymns and maybe some southern gospel styled songs. Was I ever surprised when the service began with a big "YEEHAW" and a band wearing cowboy hats and boots took the stage!

A young lady sang out front of the band. She had tight blue jeans and an even tighter pink knit top, with pink cowboy hat. The song she sang was no doubt about Jesus. But for the life of me, I can't remember it. I wonder why?

I'm not blaming the young lady. My thoughts are my fault. But when we pander so much to people that worship becomes just a gimmick, we are profaning the sacred things of God and merely entertaining each other. Needless to say, that Saturday evening I told that pastor, "Sorry, but I can't come to lead here".

While I admit that's an extreme example, it is the natural end of putting our convenience and preference on the throne in worship. If worship has to be done your way, you're not worshipping God.

You're just worshipping your style of worship.

What can we learn from these raiders of the lost Ark?

In worship, God desires passionate participation

In order to please God and fulfill His requirements, the priests had to work up a sweat! Likewise, in the Bible worship covers the full gamut of human emotions. The Biblical instrumentation is packed with loud stringed instruments and percussion - most everything but the kitchen sink!

So how in the world have we turned it into something so formal and restrained? That kind of worship is reflective of our hearts, not God's.

Notice that God wasn't satisfied until His people participated in moving the Ark. Sitting back and letting some ox do the heavy lifting was not allowed. Perhaps we ought to remember that when we sit back and let the worship team on stage do all the work while we sit silently.

In worship, we do things HIS WAY

Freedom of worship is not a license to do whatever you want. Many people use "freedom" as their excuse to disrupt a service or turn everyone's attention to them. I've had people use a tambourine they brought with them like a battering ram to beat a service into submission.

Our nation's consumer mentality has taken over many of our churches. While it's fine to try and move impediments to people attending church out of the way, we must never put our "cart before the ox"! Don't enable your congregation to believe the ultimate goal of worship is to please them.

What we want is secondary to what is good for the entire congregation. Our individual freedom of worship should never be allowed to infringe upon others. And we must never forget that what we want is of little importance in the light of what is desired by God Almighty.

Creativity in worship is wonderful. God surely delights in the imagination and variety all of His children bring to worship, from every culture and tongue. But there is one thing that is the foundation for how we worship: the Word of God. Every creative innovation or personal preference must bow to that standard.

While God is a loving Father, we should be truly fearful of doing worship in a way that might displease Him. How easily we assume upon the Lord, that He will wink at disobedience and let us make worship into something that honors us instead of Him. How quickly we assume our desires must be His.

The most important question should be: is our worship carried on the shoulders of obedience and passion, or a convenient ox cart of what's comfortable and preferred for us?

Isn't He worthy of the highest praise we can offer, not just whatever we feel comfortable with? If not, we're putting the cart before the horse. As David discovered, the cost is not worth the trouble.

TALENT'S NOT ENOUGH

I invited a non-Christian friend of mine, who had rarely if ever been to a church, to my Sunday service once. After the service, I asked him how he liked it. I'll never forget his response.

"Here's my 'review' of this morning: I liked the sermon ok, but I really enjoyed the 'warm-up act' before it most of all!"

He was dead serious. He didn't understand the purpose of the music at all, other than to prep folks for the 'headliner' who'd deliver the sermon. To him, it was all entertainment. And when you think about it, that's how someone who is unsaved probably should respond. He didn't come that day expecting to encounter a real God, he simply wanted "religious entertainment".

The sad problem is that is all some of God's people think the worship music is as well: just a warmup for the main event. They want something enjoyable that might move them, but nothing that might change them. And they see the "worship leader" as nothing more than a Christian entertainer.

When you look at church that way, it's no wonder people with musical gifts see us as just an opportunity to show off what they can do. Sunday morning is a talent show, and they're ready to take the stage and wow us. But God has a completely different idea of what a worship leader should be…

…and He absolutely refuses to give His blessing to anything less!

Some of this is a fault in the training of our worship leaders. As churches have moved farther away from a seminary trained Music Minister and more to part-time personnel, the Biblical paradigm of worship ministry has fallen by the wayside. Some have been trained vocally and instrumentally, but not theologically. Because of this error, we have attracted more performers than worshippers onto the platforms of our churches.

I believe it's time we clearly define what a worship leader should be, and what qualifications should be held up as an example to follow.

Worship Leaders are a PRIORITY to God

If God has called you to be a music minister, or to sing a solo in church, or even to just sing in the choir, you need to know that you have a noble calling. God never meant the worship leader to be the Doctor Feelgood of the church.

As I've mentioned in this book, I Chronicles 25 is an important passage regarding worship. It describes where King David was putting his kingdom in order for the eventual passing of the crown to his son Solomon. Some of his priorities were to prepare for the building of the Temple by his son, and to take stock of the nation's military defense.

However, he seems to stray off into a seemingly unimportant area. King David and some of his leaders are picking out the choir and orchestra members!

Most church music ministries would not seem worthy of the time and attention of a nation's Commander in Chief. And yet King David himself was working on it, along with his top advisers. Clearly, David saw worship leading as a priority in a way that few churches see it today.

Worship Leaders are PREACHING THROUGH MUSIC

But I was stunned by another detail. The first, second, and third verses of that chapter do not refer to the musicians as volunteers who "play" their instruments, but as appointees that must "prophecy" with music. In the Bible, those with the gift of "prophesy" are called to boldly proclaim forth the truth of God's Word.

In verse 3, it mentions that Jeduthun "prophesied with a harp to give thanks and to praise the Lord." Other translations say that he accompanied himself as he prophesied, which sounds to me like he was singing to instrumental accompaniment. The term "to prophecy" sounds pretty much like the same proclaiming of truth that the word "preaching" implies.

At that moment the confusion I had felt over my gifting went away, and I realized that God had indeed called me to "preach the Gospel"... but to preach it with music! I don't believe He ever intended church music programs to be the mere entertainment many have become. Music should not just calm and soothe, it should also convict and challenge at times. Just one listen to the prophetic music of the late Keith Green would tell you that God can convict through a sermon in song as well as through a sermon in spoken words.

In fact, the passage in I Chronicles 25 would include what we worship leaders do as a high-level spiritual activity, since they were said to be "prophesying" on their instruments. In the choir and praise team, we are called in essence to be "preachers" of the Word with our singing voices and our instruments. Our "preaching" can evidence the same power of the Holy Spirit that we see changing hearts later in our pastor's spoken Word.

Worship Leaders must be COMMITTED

I've occasionally had people say they were thinking about joining the choir, but when they realized the amount of commitment I expected from them they decided to pass on it. While I hate for them to miss the tremendous fellowship we have, I don't regret their decision not to join. To be in our choir or orchestra should be, by definition, a "high calling". If you are in front of a congregation each Sunday, you should have a higher level of commitment than your average church attender.

Speaking of "attenders", coming to church regularly is an entry-level requirement for worship leaders. If you are unwilling to attend weekly services, you lack the spiritual maturity to lead worship. Each week, what you do in our worship service is the spiritual equivalent of what a soldier does in the heat of battle. But instead of fighting to take ground, you are fighting to take back the souls of men!

Commitment to rehearsals is also a non-negotiable. We all deal with unexpected sicknesses and travel, but being engaged at regular rehearsals is a must. If you are not willing to put in the work, you do not take worship leading seriously. Notice that Psalm 33: 3 says we are to "play skillfully". To do that, you must work and rehearse. And I believe God will not anoint an uncommitted yet talented vocalist the same way He will someone who has made worship a priority.

Bottom line: if we want Him to bless our worship, we'd better be willing to put in the work!

Worship Leaders live HOLY LIVES

As a musician, I've had the privilege to work with some incredibly talented people. I've been musical directors for Broadway veterans and played in wonderful orchestras. So honestly, I'm no longer incredibly impressed with mere talent.

But one of the saddest things I've noticed is singers and musicians who make their living performing Christian music in churches, but whose lives do not reflect Christians values. I've also noticed some regular church members who think their spiritual life, or lack of it, didn't affect them as a worship leader. They felt qualified to step onto a platform and lead, even when living in open rebellion to the Word of God.

How in the world could they feel qualified to lead when living an unholy life? Quite simply, they believed all that mattered was their talent.

Of course, none of us is perfect. We all lead out of brokenness as imperfect vessels. However, that is quite different from living in open, unrepentant sin. I've had worship team members who were engaging in premarital sex, abusing illegal substances, and mistreating their spouses…yet they were shocked when I suggested they should step out of ministry and let God work in their lives. They seemed to think their talent made them indispensable to our team, when their sin actually made them temporarily unusable to the Holy Spirit.

When we lead worship, we want something to happen that is more than just the sum of our combined musical gifts. We want God to take our musical offering, humble as it may be, and add his spiritual anointing to it. That anointing gives worship power beyond just affecting the congregation emotionally. God's anointing gives worship the ability to spiritually transform the lives of people in our services.

With God's anointing on us, our worship can work wonders. But with unrepentant sin in our hearts, God will refuse to work through us. Our services will be nothing more than religious entertainment. The results will be only what we can do in our own strength. Lives won't be changed, miracles won't happen.

We will be like the Holy of Holies in the Temple of Jesus' day – looking great on the outside, but behind the curtain there's no Spirit of God resting on the Ark of the Covenant. All the religious trappings, but those trappings merely cover the fact God is nowhere near them.

Understand that when you walk out on the risers or play in the band this Sunday, you are not just entertainers. You are not just musicians, and you are not the "spoonful of sugar" that helps the message go down. You are warriors and preachers and prophets, and you have a holy calling!

Don't ever sell yourself short, and don't ever strive to be anything less! Because you are not merely "singers" performing for the entertainment of a congregation. You are worship leaders lighting a fire of passion amid the congregation, leading in spiritual warfare against the forces of evil around us.

Best of all, as we join our voices and instruments together, we bring God the greatest pleasure He can experience: the sound of all His children's voices singing as one to celebrate their Father.

When we do that, we touch on the only true wonder this world has left to offer. All others have either faded away or pale by comparison. And in our worship services on earth, we get a taste of the immeasurable wonder we will one day experience standing physically in His presence, basking in His radiance, and living for all eternity in His love.

Praise the Lord!

ABOUT DAVE

Dave is a husband, father, and pastor with the heart of a storyteller. He's an author, performer, composer, and playwright.

David Gipson is most recently the creator of the award-winning show *Pollyanna – A New Musical*, based on the classic novel by Eleanor H. Porter. He also received a 2005 BMI award for his music written for television. He is a member of the Dramatists Guild of America, and has written several original musicals that have been produced across the U.S.

Dave earned a Master of Divinity from Luther Rice Seminary in Lithonia, GA. He has served churches across the southeastern U.S., but also in Chicago and pastored in the St Louis inner city. He has also planted churches in SW Florida, with an expertise of reaching artists and creatives.

Best of all, he is the husband to his wonderful wife Dawn, the father of six beautiful children and foster father of many more.

Made in the USA
Middletown, DE
07 September 2024

60581582R00080